VIEWS OF 18TH-CENTURY RUSSIA

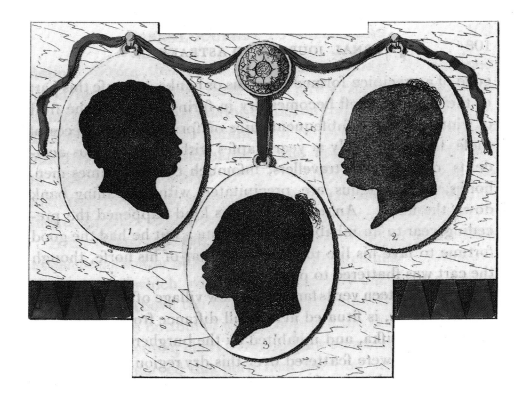

TRAVELS IN 18TH CENTURY RUSSIA

COSTUMES, CUSTOMS, HISTORY

BY

P.S. PALLAS
ROBERT JOHNSTON
AND
W. MILLER

FOREWORD BY

SIR FITZROY MACLEAN

STUDIO EDITIONS
LONDON

PUBLISHER'S NOTE

TRAVELS in 18th CENTURY RUSSIA has been compiled from extracts
taken from three sources: Travels Through the Southern Provinces of the
Russian Empire in the Years 1793 and 1794, by Professor P.S. Pallas,
Volumes I and II; Travels Through Part of the Russian Empire and the
Country of Poland: Along the Southern Shores of the Baltic, by Robert
Johnston, 1815; and The Costume of the Russian Empire, published in
1803, by W. Miller.

This edition published by Studio Editions
Princess House, 50 Eastcastle Street,
London W1N 7AP, England.

ISBN 1 85170 280 6

This book was edited and designed for
Studio Editions by Morgan Samuel Editions, London.

Printed and bound in Hong Kong

CONTENTS

FOREWORD

BY SIR FITZROY MACLEAN

FOR RUSSIA THE 18TH CENTURY MARKED, in more ways than one, a watershed. After a longish period of relative stagnation, the Russians were abruptly hauled into it and out of the Middle Ages by that larger-than-life character Peter the Great. Peter combined the roles of empire-builder and social reformer in a truly Russian tradition that had originated a couple of centuries earlier with Ivan the Terrible and was to be repeated a couple of centuries later, with equal gusto, by Josip Vissarionovich Stalin, who, recognising in Peter a kindred spirit, aptly dubbed him the First Bolshevik.

It was Peter, who, returning from a tour of Western Europe, forced his reluctant nobles to shave their traditional beards and exchange their antiquated Muscovite kaftans for the latest in masculine fashions from London and Paris, to build themselves, too, at their own expense, splendid new classical palaces with which to adorn his new Western-style capital on the banks of the River *Neva* – his "Window on the West" as he liked to call it. It was Peter, finally, who, proclaiming Russia an Empire and himself its first Emperor, set out, following once again in the footsteps of Ivan the Terrible, to extend its frontiers north, south, east and west. Having built up a powerful fleet and a well-trained, well-equipped standing army, he broke through to the Baltic and to the Black Sea, at the same time foreshadowing future conquests by pushing down to the Caucasus and the Caspian and across Siberia into Central Asia. By the end of his reign, Russia was a European power in the fullest sense of the word and by any standards a force to be reckoned with.

During the next three decades, under Peter's widow Catherine, his niece Anna and his fun-loving daughter Elizabeth, the process of Westernization continued apace. But it was not until the second half of the century that the Russians took their next great leap forward. In 1762, Peter's mantle was consciously and enthusiastically assumed by his German-born great-niece by marriage, Catherine, who, having with the help of the Imperial Guards quickly disposed of her unattractive and ineffectual husband, ascended the Imperial throne as Empress in her own right.

During the 34 years of her reign, Catherine the Great, as she understandably came to be called, added more territory to the Russian Empire than Peter himself – more indeed, than any Russian ruler since Ivan the Terrible. By the turn of the century, after Catherine had died and been succeeded in 1796 by her strange-looking and mentally unstable son Paul, a child of dubious paternity, Russia had absorbed most of Poland, taken Odessa and the Black Sea Littoral, including the Crimea from Turkey, and reaching out across the Caucasus, formally annexed the ancient Christian Kingdom of Georgia.

With the Napoleonic Wars, Russia, under Catherine's grandson Alexander, entered a new and important phase of her Imperial development. In 1801 the unfortunate Paul had been murdered by the officers of his Palace Guard, acting in semi-collusion with his enigmatic and equivocal son. In 1812, an attempt by Alexander to do a deal with Napoleon at his allies' expense ended, in much the same way as Stalin's similar attempt to appease Hitler, when Napoleon, like Hitler in 1941, invaded Russia. But, from a war between emperors, the ensuing conflict, again like that of 1941, was to become a war of national resistance against a foreign invader. Rising to the occasion, the Russian people held the enemy's advance and in the end drove the alien invaders from their country. In March 1814, Alexander, after leading the allied advance into France, entered Paris at the head of his victorious army. Having played a leading part in the war, he was to play a leading part in the peace settlement which followed it and which, not unnaturally, brought his country substantial gains.

Such, in very broad lines, is the historical background to the fascinating journeys which form the subject of this book. Undertaken in a spirit of enquiry and investigation worthy of the Age of Enlightenment, they carried the authors to regions often newly conquered, very largely uninhabited by non-Russians and for the most part unfamiliar to the reading public. For Russia this had been an era of expansion and discovery, of opening up to new ideas which barely a century later would convulse and ultimately remould the Empire which "the first Bolshevik" had so proudly proclaimed 200 years before.

The greater part of this book is concerned with travels undertaken in the years 1793 and 1794 by Professor PS Pallas of St Petersburg, by special permission, we are told, from the Empress Catherine, herself a renowned patroness of science and the arts. They took him through "the Southern Provinces of Russia" to the fringes of the Caucasus and finally to the newly conquered Crimea, which he was to study in some detail and where he later very sensibly made his home. Though not a Russian by birth, the Professor had spent most of his working life in Russia, ending up as an Imperial State Counsellor. His journey, he tells us, was undertaken partly for reasons of health and partly to escape what he calls the "unpleasant bustle" and "artificial society" of the capital, but also to supplement information gathered on an earlier journey and to observe such changes as had occurred in the interval. He was accompanied by his wife and daughter and also, very fortunately for us, by Herr Geissler, a "skilful artist" from Leipzig. Though primarily a botanist and zoologist, Professor Pallas was clearly more of a polymath in the style of his great contemporary Lomonosov, the founder of Moscow University, and therefore always ready to turn his lively and enquiring mind to the study of any likely subject that came his way, whether ethnology, etymology, geology or gastronomy.

Mr Johnston, whose comments and accompanying illustrations occupy the last quarter of the book, was evidently one of those itinerant Britons who ranged around the world in the early 19th century, choosing, for his own part, to visit the Baltic, St Petersburg and Moscow in the Spring of 1814, with Napoleon, for the time being, safely on Elba. His account of Moscow, two years after the great fire and still very largely in ruins, is particularly interesting. Though enthusiastic about much that he saw, notably the "enchanted" city of St Petersburg, rising miraculously from the surrounding marshes, he pulls no punches when it comes to people. The soldiers of a regiment of Bashkirs he found occupying Hamburg he calls "the most shocking ruffians which the imagination can picture". Of the Jewesses of Lithuania he sourly remarks that "there never was a more perfect antidote to love". The native Lithuanians he dismisses as "abject, gross, indolent and dispiriting". And of the Kitaigorod in Moscow he writes "idleness and sloth, knavery and superstition are the offensive appearances of this singular place". Nor can he reconcile himself to the openly incestuous practices prevailing in Novgorod the Great.

Having myself spent a good deal of time over the last half century travelling through all the Russias, I must admit to a certain fellow feeling for both travellers. There is something about Russia which makes all travel there endlessly fascinating; there is a perpetual sense of uncertainty, of the unexpected. You never know what is – or what is not – waiting for you around the corner: sometimes, it is true, an unpleasant surprise or disappointment, but more often an unexpected treat – something you had no idea could possibly happen. It is for this reason that I return there as often as I do and, after literally scores of visits, I can truthfully say that I rarely come away disappointed.

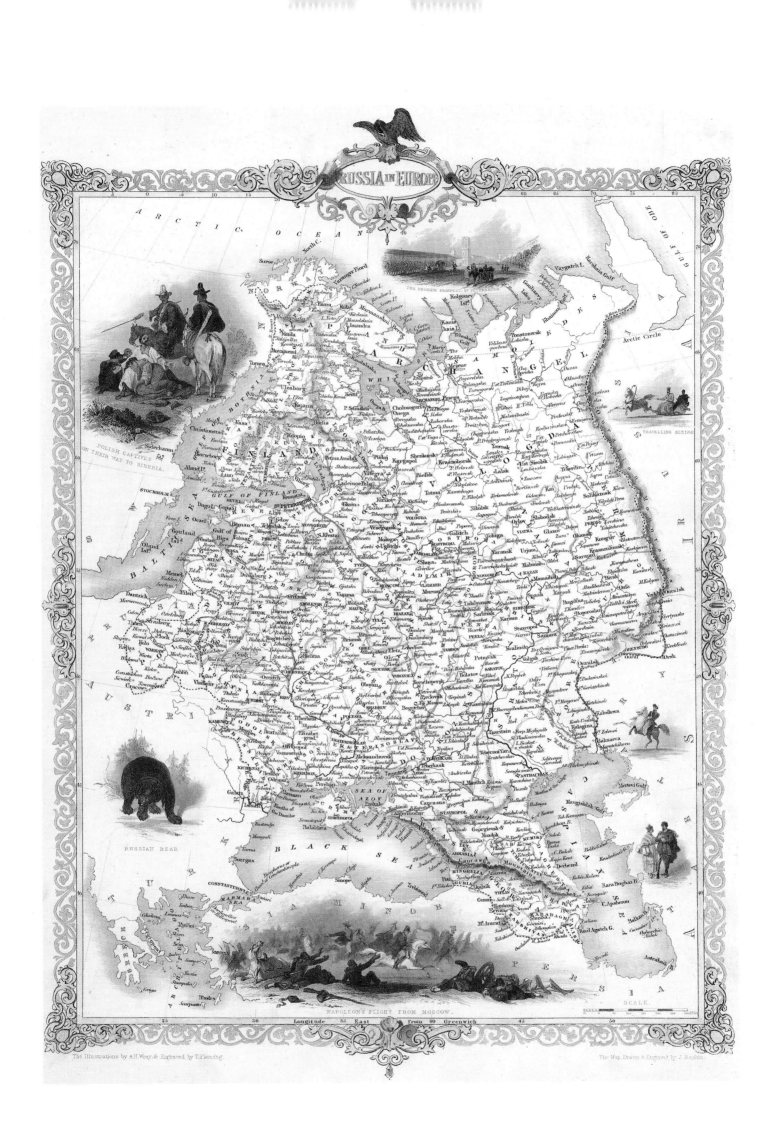

RUSSIA IN EUROPE

POLISH CAPTIVES ON THEIR WAY TO SIBERIA.

THE NEWSKI PROSPECT, ST PETERSBURG.

TRAVELLING SLEDGE

RUSSIAN BEAR

NAPOLEON'S FLIGHT FROM MOSCOW.

SCALE

The Illustrations by A.H.Wray & Engraved by T.Fleming.

The Map, Drawn & Engraved by J. Rapkin.

This map and the map on the previous page are taken from *The Illustrated Atlas of the Nineteenth-Century World*, edited by Montgomery Martin and first published in 1851

KAMTCHATKAN DOGS.

INTRODUCTION

FROM THE MOMENT THAT EUROPEAN TRAVELLERS first set foot in Russia and began to write about what they found, they started to create, rather than dispel, the myths that enshrouded this vast land. They assumed that Russia was a mysterious and barbaric land. As the Englishman Samuel Collins, writing in the late 17th century, said, "the Russians are a people who differ from all other nations of the world in most of their actions".

And this was part of the myth. The Western observers, riddled with prejudice, relished the idea of a huge and untamed country inhabited by primitive peoples who were weighed down by their own ignorance, by a harsh climate and by an oppressive system of government. They could not help thinking that Russia was inferior to Europe because it was not like Europe. So what they saw was conditioned by what they already believed, and their reactions range from curiosity and wonder to condescension, pity and disgust. Yet, whatever preconceptions they reveal, many of these early writings are wonderfully vivid and informative; witty, entertaining, and sympathetic.

However, a few travellers did attempt to be objective, and Professor Pallas, extracts from whose writings form Sections I and II of this book, was one of them. He writes carefully and painstakingly about everything he encounters: about the landscape – the plains and the large, slow rivers flowing south to the Caspian and Black seas, the wild and inhospitable Caucasus Mountains and the beautiful flower-filled valleys and mountainous coasts of the Crimea; about the barbarous rural settlements; about the people, whose appearance and customs fascinate him while at the same time provoking him to express the hope that they could be tamed and brought more effectively under the control of the Russian government; about the towns that shock him, yet are sufficiently picturesque to attract.

Ostensibly, Pallas is merely writing down his observations for the interest and use of Empress Catherine the Great, so although he has a practical attitude towards a particularly lush river valley, a spectacular stretch of coastline, a notoriously bloodthirsty tribe of people – would they make good farmland, a good harbour, good soldiers, if tamed? – the crammed pages do not betray much in the way of prejudice or sentimentality. The picture he presents is full of detail, and full of integrity. In fact, Pallas is one of the few writers about Russia who did not fall wholly for the myth of its mysteriousness.

The other main author represented in this book is an Oxford graduate called Robert Johnston. He saw Russia 30 years later than

12

Pallas, and writes in a spirit that reflects the turmoil that was Europe during those years: the Naopleonic Wars.

Western attitudes towards Russia had been changed by the Napoleonic threat to European civilization, and whereas Professor Pallas was a German civil servant employed by the Russian imperial government with a job to do, Johnston felt free to be more subjective and express himself more freely. He adopts the literary tone of his times, giving passionate voice to his opinions and unhesitatingly adding touches of colour to his observations. His descriptions are vivid, and are mostly of people and places; he is not an amateur geologist or botanist, as were Pallas and many other travellers.

But Johnston shared with other Western onlookers the conviction that Russia was an unfathomable mystery. Even though he readily and enthusiastically concedes that Europe owes a huge debt to Mother Russia for her part in the overthrow of the tyrant Napoleon, he finds it hard to admire the culture and the customs of her people because he does not understand them. So he says that the language "is spoken by the natives with extreme quickness and has a soft hissing sound ... Russian literature must ever be cramped until their language is altered. Independently of any other reasons their authors have too much verbiage in the very structure of their sentences and words, and even in the characters of their alphabet there is a kind of barbarism."

However, where Johnston is more subjective than Pallas he is also more ebullient and entertaining. He does not solve the enigma of Russia but he writes about it with a bold enthusiasm that could not have failed to freshen to outlook of even the most obdurate Western European.

One of the reasons for the difficulty that Westerners had in understanding Russia was that they were obsessed with the question of whether Russia was part of Europe. They judged her achievements from a Western point of view, and often in ignorance. So even Madame de Stael could suggest in 1811 that "poetry, eloquence, literature are not yet found in Russia".

Politically, by the 18th century and the reign of Peter the Great, Russia was certainly a power in Europe, and Peter himself was determined to westernize where he could. For Europeans the enlightened Emperor of Russia (as he now called himself, preferring this more European-sounding title to that of "Tsar of Muscovy"), who so conspicuously admired and emulated their civilization, was thus a hero, and the poet James Thomson, the author of the words of "Rule Britannia", wrote with similar enthusiasm:

Immortal Peter! First of monarchs! He
His stubborn country tamed, – her rocks, her fens

13

Her floods, her seas, her ill-submitting sons;
And while the fierce barbarian he subdued,
To more exalted soul he raised the man.

Since Russia herself, under Peter the Great and later under Catherine the Great, was so eager to adopt European ideas and culture, it is not surprising that European visitors should have taken a patronizing attitude towards their imitators. If Russia was European after all, and the numerous manifestations of the Asian presence there were the result of an unfortunate episode in history that could now be brushed aside as an aberration, then the benefits of European civilization were Russia's rightful inheritance anyway. It was time, the visitors thought, for Russia to do some catching up.

The new city of St Petersburg proclaimed Peter the Great's vision of Russia as a civilized, European nation, and became a great tourist attraction. Visitors marvelled at its beauty, its extravagant architecture, and the speed with which it had risen up out of the swamps of the *Neva* delta. Robert Johnston describes it in rapturous terms: he wakes on his first morning in the imperial capital, having arrived there at night, to be greeted by a view of the towers of the city, "their domes glittering in the rising sun and throwing their rich tints on the placid bosom of the river Neva; not pen, nor pencil, nor tongue, can give adequate effect to the glorious *coup d'oeil*. It is more like the bright vision of an eastern night, more like the light which gilds the poet's dream than the cold morning realities of the common life."

It was seen as a wonder of the world. And yet, in the midst of elegance, refinement, good taste, and all the other virtues that had supposedly rubbed off on Russia thanks to her contact with Europe, there were the Russians, who apparently were unchanged – unenlightened, poor barbarians still. Foreigners loved to dwell on the ignorance and vices of the Russian "boor", his slavish religious devotion and his ill-treatment of his women. However, by the end of the 18th century many travellers to unfamiliar countries – Africa and the New World as well as Russia – had come across the appealing idea of the "noble savage", and so could be expected to regard apparently primitive peoples with more sympathy, if not genuine understanding. So Robert Johnston says of the Russian serf, "Treat him with occasional flattery, and particularly allow him the freedom of speech, and he becomes obliging and indefatigable."

Travellers to Russia writing at the time of Pallas and Johnston therefore felt ambivalent towards its status as a European nation: on the one hand were all the trappings of a civilization that they themselves stood for; on the other were the oppressed masses, whose sufferings were compounded by a climate that has defeated armies when all else has failed.

14

In reading the descriptions that were written of Russia and her people we share the excitement, awe and sometimes apprehension that were felt by these early travellers. There were many of them, and there are many accounts of their experiences. Professor Pallas and Robert Johnston are both typical of travel writers of their time. Pallas was one of several German professors imported by Catherine the Great to carry out research for her and provide her with information about her vast empire. He held the office of Counsellor of State at the Imperial Court, and travelled around Russia recording what he saw was his job. Robert Johnston was an educated Englishman, who, like many of his contemporaries, was attracted by the challenge of the "Northern Tour", a more exciting version of the 18th-century Grand Tour, which was a well-worn theme by now.

Views of 18th-Century Russia is a series of extracts from the writings of these two men. The book falls naturally into three sections. The first two are from Pallas's *Travels through the Southern Provinces of the Russian Empire in the Years 1793 and 1794*. In this two-volume work Pallas describes his long journey from St Petersburg to the southern Volga, on into the Caucasus Mountains and then to the Crimea. The third section of *Views of 18th-Century Russia* is taken from Robert Johnston's *Travels Through Part of the Russian Empire and the Country of Poland; Along the Southern Shores of the Baltic*, which was published in 1815.

Both writers illustrated their travels, and Professor Pallas in particular refers often to "my draughtsman" who accompanied him and sketched away while Pallas hunted for plants and fossils. The evocative and very beautiful engravings of cities, churches, palaces, landscapes and the peoples of Russia that resulted have been reproduced here.

Alongside the descriptions and anecdotes of these two writers have been included extracts from *The Costume of the Russian Empire*, published in 1803. Its exquisite engravings were based on a series executed in St Petersburg from 1776 to 1779 "at the desire of the late Empress" (Catherine the Great), and cover the whole of the Russian empire as it then was. The descriptions of the costumes were gathered from the descriptions of a number of ethnographers of the time, among them Professor Pallas, by W Miller, a London publisher. Many of the nations covered by this book are mentioned by our two travellers, or inhabit the regions through which they pass, and are included here in their appropriate place.

SECTION I

FROM MOSCOW TO TAGANROG

PROFESSOR PALLAS SET OUT FROM ST PETERSBURG with his wife and daughter – who are rarely mentioned in his Travels – at the beginning of 1793. The weather was uncharacteristically mild as they travelled to Moscow, where they stayed for a short time before setting off on the road south – through Penza, via Saratov, to Tzaritzin. As the weather grew colder, however, the small party was often able to travel along the ice of the Volga in sledges.

Pallas takes in every detail of the journey, giving us a remarkably vivid impression of the cold, windswept landscape: the snowdrifts, the forlorn winter birds and the frozen rivers. Then the weather changes and the thaw begins; melt-water rushes into the rivers everywhere, and the first flowers of spring appear. From Tzaritzin, Pallas travels to Astrakhan on the Caspian Sea, and spends much of the summer exploring the southern Volga and collecting rare

plants. *En route* he becomes fascinated by the strange Kalmuks and primitive Tartars, describing them in great detail.

The next stage of the journey takes Pallas into the Caucasus Mountains – the region is notoriously dangerous, yet he is surprisingly sanguine when describing his travels through it. He explores the mountains, continues his plant-hunting, and writes fascinating descriptions of the peoples who native inhabitants – Circassians, Ingushians, Cossacks, and Nagays. Leaving the Caucasus Mountains in October, his party makes its way to the port of Taganrog on the Sea of Azov, then travels on to Mariupol, which Pallas describes as a Greek town with houses constructed in the Grecian style. Here, as at Taganrog, and earlier at Astrakhan, evocative portrayals convey the contrast between Pallas's appreciation of the life-enhancing hustle and bustle of a boisterous commercial port and his deprecatory frisson of disapproval at the raffishness on display.

From Mariupol, Pallas sets off for the Crimean peninsula, which is the subject of Section II of this volume.

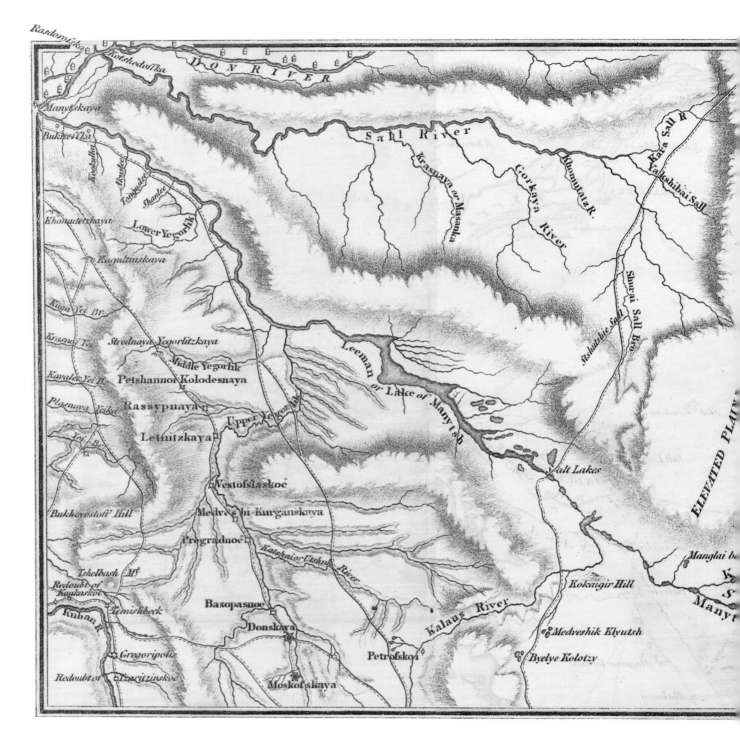

The country of the Lower Volga, showing the extensive plains, or
steppes, situated between the Caspian Sea and the Sea of Azov.

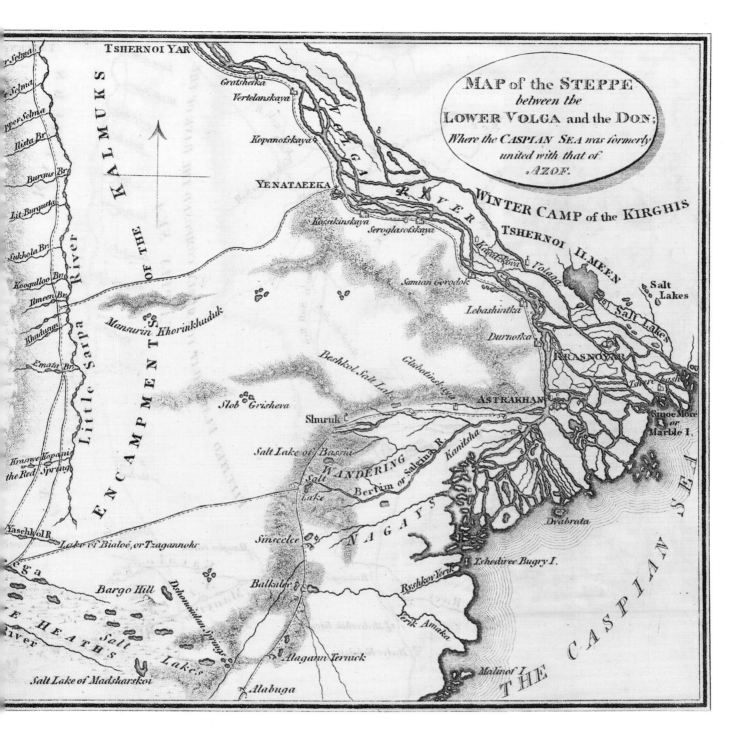

TSHERNOI YAR

MAP of the STEPPE
between the
LOWER VOLGA and the DON;
Where the CASPIAN SEA was formerly
united with that of
AZOF.

WINTER CAMP of the KIRGHIS

TSHERNOI ILMEEN

Gratsheika

Vertelanskaya

Kopanofskaya

YENATAEEKA

Kassikinskaya

Seroglasofskaya

Medatsova Volaga

Salt
Lakes

Samian Gorodok

Salt Lakes

Lebashintka

Durnofka

KRASNOYAR

Mansurin Khorinkhuduk

Beshkol Salt Lake

Glubotinskoi

Tshere bashi

Slob Grisheva

ASTRAKHAN

Shuruk

Snoe More
or
Marble I.

Salt Lake of Basna

WANDERING

Salt
Lake

Berfum or Salcina R.

Kanitsha

Sinseelce

NAGAYS

Dvabrata

Yaschkol R

Lake of Bialoé, or Tzagannohr

Balkaler

Tshediree Bugry I.

Ryshkov Yerik

Bargo Hill

Dsharmilhan Springs

Yerik Amaka

Salt Lakes

Alagann Ternick

Malinof I.

THE CASPIAN SEA

Salt Lake of Madsharskoi

Alabuga

KALMUKS

ENCAMPMENTS OF THE

Little Sarpa River

r Selma

e Selma

pper Selma

Ilista Br.

Burgus Br.

Lit Burgusta

Sukhola Br.

Koogulloo Br.

Ilmeen Br.

Khudyagn

Emata Br.

Krasnye Kopanie
the Red Springs

ga

HEATHS

River

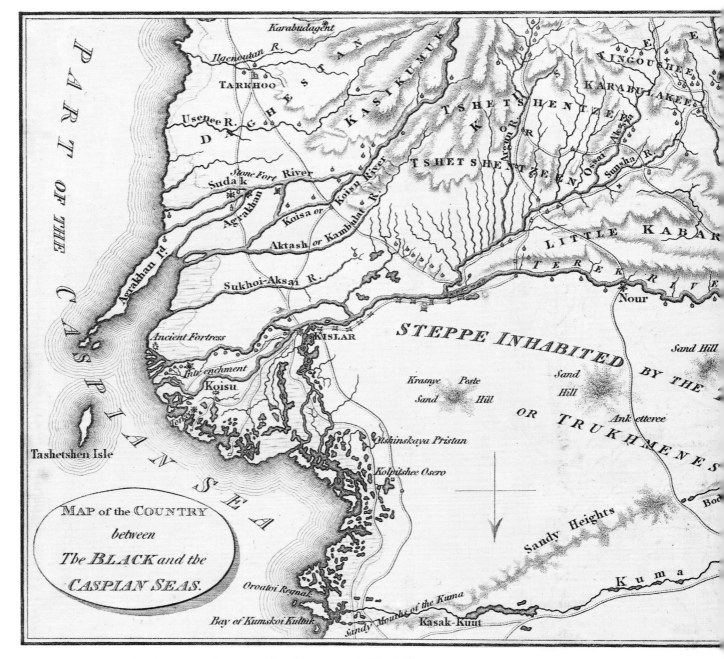

The mountains of the Caucasus between the Caspian and Black Seas.

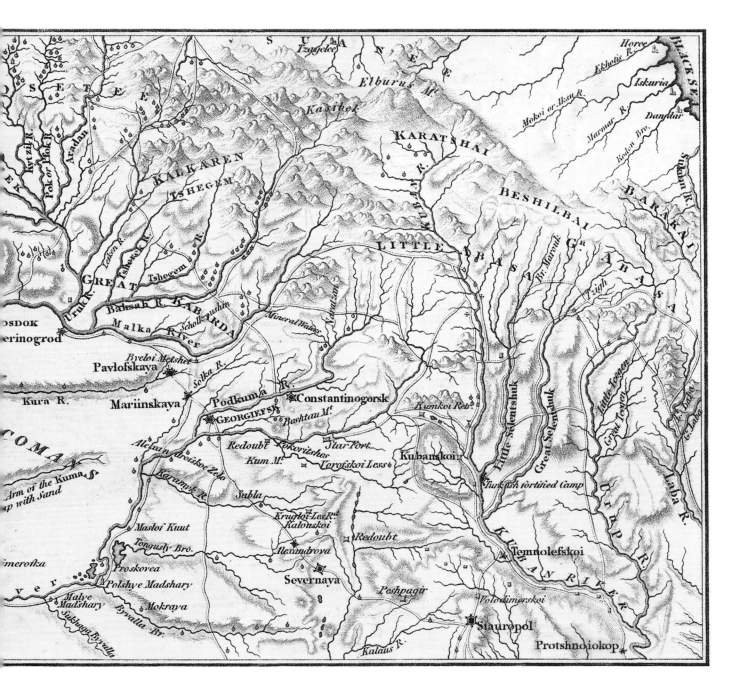

FROM THE HOLY CITY TO PENZA

FEBRUARY 1793

THE WEATHER HAD BEEN UNUSUALLY MILD during winter, so that we arrived at Moscow on the commencement of the thaw. Moscow has during the last twenty years been much improved not only in the magnificence of its buildings, and the refinement of taste and manners, but in the luxury of its inhabitants. Every object we behold here is in a certain degree gigantic. Several palaces, in particular, are of a vast size, resembling castles; and they are inhabited by hundreds of servants, who are born in a state of vassalage.

The foundling hospital is one of the most extensive charitable institutions in the world. Some of the country residences are planned, and the architecture finished, in a magnificent style. But the institution particularly deserving notice is the new Assembly House of the Nobility, which during winter is visited by at least one thousand persons of rank, of both sexes, who appear at the balls and masquerades in very superb dresses.

Several indispensable arrangements for our journey detained us at Moscow till 19th February, then we directed our journey by way of Penza to Saratov. The whole country through which we passed is embellished with numerous villages, belonging chiefly to noblemen, and is one of the most fertile grain provinces of the Russian empire.

Despite this, agriculture is most shamefully neglected and the boors live in miserable smoky huts, and in the most disgusting state of uncleanliness.

Penza, on account of its widespread cultivation, has scarcely any wild animals excepting those of the forest. A particular species, or mongrel variety, of the domestic cat, engaged a considerable share of my attention. It had kittened three young ones that exactly resembled each other and lived alone in the village of Nikolskoi, in the district of Insara, on a nobleman's estate, and often retired to a young forest behind a garden laid out in the English style. The domestics had remarked that this cat was absent during the rutting season; and it was also reported that she formerly had kittens of the common kind, which she devoured a few days after their birth.

A peculiar species of the domestic cat. In the upper part of the engraving is the coat of arms of the town and district of Mokshan, showing the two battle-axes of the Mordvines.

A MESTSCHERAKIAN WOMAN

THIS TARTARIAN TRIBE INHABIT THE SAME part of the country as the Bashkirs, with whom they are very much intermixed, and to whom they paid a small annual sum, as possessors of the soil, when they first settled among them. This was in the beginning of the 15th century. When the Bashkirs revolted in the year 1735, the Mestscheriaks remained faithful to the government, in consequence of which they were freed from their tribute.

They are in general more enlightened than the Bashkirs, better Muslims, and more faithful subjects. They do not lead a wandering life, but are chiefly employed in the care of their cattle and their bees, which they cultivate as assiduously as the Bashkirs themselves; they do not, however, altogether neglect agriculture. The men dress exactly like the Bashkirs, but the women in some respects differ, particularly in their flat bonnets, which they ornament with pieces of money and glass beads; long pieces of cord also hang down, and are covered with plates of silver, or white iron.

THE WINTER ROAD FROM PENZA TO TZARITZIN

MARCH 1793

WE LEFT PENZA WITH A GRATEFUL sense of the hospitality we had experienced in that town. We arrived at the brook *Kondaly*, 24 versts from Penza. All the names of rivers and brooks here are of Tartarian derivation, and the term *kondaly*, which signifies the water of the beavers, is a proof of the former existence of that curious animal in these regions. In these and many other open regions, travellers are exposed to great danger in winter, on account of the drifts of snow that cover the roads, and are pointed out by marks of brushwood, or young trees.

The town of Saratov, where we arrived on 12th March, has increased much in trade and population, and consequently in regular buildings, since the establishment of viceroyalties, or provincial governments. I was in hopes of hailing the approach of spring at Saratov; but I found the ground covered with deep snow, and the frost, which had succeeded the mild weather of February, was of such intensity and continuance that we were obliged to use the usual winter-road with our covered sledges.

So we continued our journey down to Tzaritzin, on the icy pavement of the Volga, which was nearly a yard thick. The continued north-west wind and severe frost were favourable, as they enabled us to travel with more expedition along the ice of the Volga. Thus at the same time I was able to examine the whole diameter of the high stratified hills which extend along the intersected right bank of the Volga, down to Tzaritzin.

This bank is formed of precipices; towards the base it is overgrown with stunted white poplar and willow trees, and is entirely inundated by the stream at high water. Near Proleika begins a stratum of yellow sand, which becomes progressively thicker, and occupies the upper part of both banks. This stratum of sandstone rises continually, and forms the Strelnye-Gory, or arrow mounts, which ascend from 10 to 15 fathoms above the Volga. The rocks on the top of the bank exhibit various extraordinary figures like busts on pedestals, which project in a row from the bank, as brick-work ornamented with a variety of vases.

The curious Strelnye-Gory rock formations forming the bank of the river Volga above Dubofka. On the river is a fishing boat with both sails and oars.

A FEMALE MORDVINE OF THE ERZIAN TRIBE

THE MORDVI ARE DIVIDED INTO TWO tribes, the Erzian and the Mokshan, and inhabit the governments of Nizney, Novgorod, Kazan, Sinbirsk, Oufa and Penza. This and the next plate exhibit a female of the Erzian tribe, while the succeeding two plates are descriptive of the Mokshan tribe.

The latter chiefly inhabit the neighbourhood of the rivers Moksha and Oka, while the former live mostly on the banks of the Volga. These nations are also derived from the Finns, although they have, from their former subjection to the Tartars, a great many Tartarian words in their language: that of each tribe was formerly very different, but they have lately become much mixed. These people are in general honest, laborious, and friendly, but very slow in their work. Since they have been under the Russian government, they employ themselves in the cultivation of the land; and they have a great dislike of living in large towns. The women employ themselves in spinning, and making their clothes.

They purchase their wives, and the common price is not more than 10 roubles, or about £2: the marriage ceremony and rejoicing continue the whole day. In the burial of their dead, they have a singular custom of meeting in all their best clothes; and have a sort of feast, of which they always leave part on the grave or coffin. Most of the people are Christians, although some still continue pagans.

A FEMALE MORDVINE OF THE ERZIAN TRIBE FROM THE BACK

THE DRESS OF A MORDVINE OF the Erzian tribe is not very different from those of Mokshan. The married women, in general, dress more than others, but there is no essential difference, except perhaps in the head-dress. They both wear drawers of linen, which reach only to their knees. Their shifts are worked and embroidered in the most fantastic manner, and fastened round their waist by a girdle; to this girdle they fix on behind a small kind of apron, very much worked, and ornamented with fringe and various kinds of tassels.

When they wish to dress as fine as they can, the women fasten on all round their girdle a very wide piece of cloth, every part of which is highly worked, and ornamented with fringe and tassels. They wear round their neck, and over their shoulders and breast, an ornament, composed of a kind of enamel, and of coins or medals. They also wear large earrings, and wear bracelets at the wrist. The elder women cover their head with a sort of cap, which fits close, and falls down behind; while the younger wear a high bonnet, narrower towards the top, and flat, ornamented with beads and embroidery in front, and with strings of beads and tassels behind.

A MORDVINE OF THE MOKSHAN TRIBE

THE DRESS OF THE WOMEN OF this tribe differs very little from that of the Erzian women. Their bonnets, which they call *panga*, are not so high as those of the latter tribe; and many of them, at least when young, wear only a worked piece of linen over their head. They also braid their hair in tresses, and mix black wool with it, in order to make it appear thicker and longer. When they wear bonnets, they fasten to the back part of them two strips of skin, very much ornamented, which come down over their shoulders to their breast.

They also dress themselves out in collars and rows of beads, which serve them by way of handkerchief, and which they call *zifks*; and to this they fasten a piece of cloth, or linen, called *siai*, reaching almost to their girdle, and closely ornamented with pieces of enamel and shells. Their shoes are made of the bark of trees; and instead of stockings, they wrap pieces of linen round their feet and legs.

AN OLD MORDVINE WOMAN OF THE MOKSHAN TRIBE

THE OLD PEOPLE OF THIS TRIBE dress their heads in a manner not very dissimilar from the young girls; they simply cover them with a piece of linen, very much worked, which takes the shape of the head, and falling down on their back, in some measure covers their hair, which is not otherwise confined but falls loose on their shoulders. Instead of an apron fastened to their girdle behind, which is worn by the Erzian tribe, the Mokshans hang a quantity of tassels half way down. To their common earrings they also fix some small tassels made of swan's down, and they put ornamental rings to different parts of their dress.

SPRING IN THE SOUTHERN VOLGA

MARCH – APRIL 1793

IN THE AFTERNOON OF 20TH MARCH we arrived at Tzaritzin, in frosty weather. The earth was still covered with deep snow and the ice on the river was solid. In former years, at this season, and in these southern regions, according to the natural vicissitudes of things, the summer fields were sown, cattle grazed on the fresh pastures and the first plants of spring used to be in full bloom. But this year the cold north-east winds, which succeeded those from the north-west, continued through the whole month of March, and the night frosts were so intense that the meridian sun could scarcely soften the earth.

At length, after a long and severe winter, two calm foggy days intervened with the new moon of April; the wind changed to the east, and brought on a permanent thaw. Thus all the snow which lay on the eastern and southern sides of the heights suddenly dissolved; the water rushed into the rivulets, and formed rapid torrents, which precipitated themselves into the Volga. We now remarked the arrival of all the birds of passage, among which were an incredible number of birds of prey, flights of swans, starlings, and geese of different kinds; the first swallows we saw on 4th April. We saw in every direction the tulip, and the mountain-saffron sprouting forth, while the first chafer and *Citillus*, or mountain-mouse, awoke from their brumal slumber. On 7th April the ice of the Volga broke up completely, the thaw being accompanied with a warm rain.

After this sudden change of the season, I began to prepare for my botanical excursions on the southern bank of the Volga; and my first journey was to the colony of evangelical brethren at Sarepta, or Sarpa, where I stayed till 18th April.

Although Sarepta had, soon after my former journey to these regions in 1773, been plundered by the rebellious bands of Pugatchev, yet I found it considerably improved, beautified, and in a state of increasing prosperity. The market-place is regular, and adorned with elegant buildings, particularly the church and the well-built mansions of the Moravians.

Sarepta, on the banks of the Sarpa, from its western side. In the foreground is the Farm; in the distance the wooded islands in the river Volga. The market-place and the principal streets are beautified with rows of poplar trees.

THE KALMUKS

APRIL 1793

THE DESERT BELOW SAREPTA, OVER WHICH we now travelled, produced a great number of early white and yellow tulips, the *Tulipa biflora* and *silvestris*. We proceeded along a steep bank, from which we beheld the low country overspread with multitudes of wild-fowl. After travelling for about 18 versts we left the Volga, and travelled over a flat steppe, on which we observed many sepulchral hillocks. We again approached the Volga, where the hip-bone of an elephant and several ivory teeth have lately been found on the precipice of the bank. A Kalmuk brought me an imperfect grinder of an old elephant, which he had found in the glen of the steppe.

On 22nd April I proceeded towards Yenatevka where we again met with Kalmuks, who are fond of passing the winter here in numerous hordes, but who in the present year had been infected by the small-pox, which was epidemic along the Volga, and obliged them to disperse; this is a disease as dreadful and destructive to them as the plague. According to the latest lists which I received, the remains of this remarkable people, who since the introduction of the provincial governments and the division of lands are confined to a more limited situation, still consists of 8229 family tents. A large related horde of Derbetes who have withdrawn themselves from this neighbourhood number 4900 hearths on the steppe of the Volga. To this number may be added about 200 baptized, free and civilized Kalmuks, who dwell in Astrakhan and its vicinity.

Frequent attempts have been made to induce the Kalmuks to form a settlement; but they are so much accustomed to uncontrolled and vagrant habits that it was only from the extreme indigence of their fugitive brethren, who have lately begun to emigrate to the province of Songary in the Chinese dominions, that their present rulers have been able to compel this unsteady people to apply themselves to agriculture and reside in settled habitations.

A Kalmuk of the lower class, with a rifle over his shoulder and a horse-whip in his hand, and a Kalmuk priest in his peculiar dress. In the background are the tents, or temporary felt huts, inhabited by that nation.

EXCURSIONS IN THE SOUTHERN VOLGA

APRIL – MAY 1793

THE KALMUKS AND THE MONGOLS ARE kindred nations, and along with the Nagays all three show the characteristic Mongolian traits which have been unchanged through the lapse of many centuries. It is proof of how strongly the Mongolian nation impress their characteristics on the people with whom they are intermixed; for instance, on the Chinese and the Russians who live beyond the Baikal.

Beyond Yenatevka the steppe becomes more sandy as it decreases, and at unequal distances displays banks of moving sand, which becomes progressively more frequent. A quantity of decayed shells are everywhere found intermixed with the sand, and some Caspian mussels in a calcined state. The dry steppe is very hilly, though it does not rise more than two or three fathoms above the level of the Volga. The low country abounds with grass, is interspersed with willows, and sown with tulips.

On 25th April I was ferried over the Solanka, as its bridge had been carried away by the flood; and thence I proceeded in a boat on the Volga to Astrakhan. To that important place, the principal seat of our Asiatic commerce, and the general magazine of fish for the whole Russian empire in Europe, I intend to return in the month of August.

From Astrakhan we headed for the city of Krasnyy Yar, which is built on an island formed by the confluence of the river Bufan with the Akhtouba and the Algara. It is intersected by several small canals, and part of the island is inundated at high water, and then the streets of even the higher parts of the town are overflowed. At such times travellers can proceed in boats directly to Astrakhan.

The city contains about 300 houses, a stone church, sufficiently large for the population of the place, and one of wood. The gardens of the inhabitants are particularly celebrated for delicious autumnal pears, and for their apples, and a large species of white onion which is much esteemed.

A Kalmuk housewife and girl, in their national dress.

A KALMUK

THE KALMUKS ARE ONE OF THE Mongol nations, and inhabit the country to the west of Astrakhan, near the shores of the Caspian Sea. Some of them also inhabit the city of Astrakhan. They are, in general, of a moderate stature, well made, but thin; their faces are remarkably flat, particularly their noses; their eyes are small and narrow, with the corners towards their temples pointing downwards; their lips are thick, their hair black, their complexions tawny, and their ears remarkably large, and standing wide from the head. In most persons of this country, the senses of feeling and taste are exceedingly dull, while those of hearing, seeing and smelling are very acute. In consequence of riding much on horseback, and their mode of sitting cross-legged, the Kalmuks are generally bow-kneed.

The outer garment of the men is very similar to that of the Poles, excepting the sleeves, which are narrow and tight on the wrist. Under this they wear a vest entirely buttoned, called *bechmet*, round which they fasten a sash. Those among them who are opulent have also a short skirt, open in front, and large pantaloons, made of linen, called *kitaika*, which reach down to the top of their boots; while the poorer sort only wear a straight pelisse fastened with a sash.

A FEMALE KALMUK

THE DRESS OF THE WOMEN DOES not differ much from that of the men, except with respect to the materials with which it is formed, and the quantity of work bestowed upon it; both of which are of a superior quality. Those who are affluent wear over the *bechmet*, a long robe of fine stuff without sleeves, while the outer garment is placed over one or both shoulders, like a cloak. This has sleeves, but they are not commonly used. Their caps are round, and have a border of fur. Those of the poor are called *macale*, and are made of stuff, so as just to cover the top of the head; while those of the rich are called *chalban*, and made of silk lined with black velvet and have generally a red tassel on top.

The Kalmuks in general, except such as reside at Astrakhan, have for their habitations a sort of tent, made of felt, and supported by a frame of wickerwork, which for strength, lightness, and ingenuity of construction are truly worthy of admiration.

A KUNDURE TARTAR ENCAMPMENT

MAY 1793

ON 20TH MAY WE ARRIVED AT an extensive low country called Karavaily in a calm evening, attended with continual flashes of lightning. In this valley were encamped numbers of Auli, or migrating hordes of the Kundure Tartars, among whom was the family of my guide Arflan, one of the most wealthy elders of that nation. We found felt tents prepared for us here, and we passed the night cheerfully for at this season the gnats are innumerable along the Volga, and allow no rest to the traveller if he is unprotected by a proper tent.

The Kundure Tartars, whom I had formerly found in peculiar felt tents, in the form of baskets, which could not be taken to pieces but were placed on poles supported by two-wheeled carriages, had now begun to dwell in huts similar to those of the Kirghis. They consist of several pieces which can be disjoined, and thus form a more capacious and convenient tent.

Each wealthy Tartar family commonly has two tents, one for the reception of their visitors, and the other appropriated to their females; besides which, according to the number of the family, they usually have one or more covered two-wheeled chariots for their wives and daughters. These chariots are painted of various colours; and on the fore-part there is commonly placed a chest, covered with ornamental tapestry, containing their best clothes. The inside of these vehicles, which are generally drawn by two oxen, is occupied by the female part of the family during their migrations. Besides these chariots they have one or more two-wheeled carts which are loaded with their tents, chests and other heavy articles. The moveables of each family remain together on their journey, and in regular order, as represented in the plate.

A rural encampment of the Kundure Tartars, who lead a wandering life on the banks of the Akhtouba. Both the Tartar and Kalmuk types of tent are shown, and also the covered chariots exclusively devoted to females.

TARTAR WOMEN

MAY 1793

THE DRESS OF THE TARTAR WOMEN and girls differs in several part-iculars from that of the other Nagay tribes. The girls wear a sort of red cap, made of the rind of trees, in the form of a bee-hive, and ornamented with pieces of tin. Corals and small pieces of coin are suspended around this head-dress. The gown is made of variegated silk stuff, has long narrow sleeves, and is adorned from the breast to the waist with tassels of tin or silver, buttons, little bells, and rings. They wear a strap or cord over the left shoulder, to which is attached a tin case, containing amulets, and usually a large shell. The women are the most inelegant beings imaginable. In summer they dress in an upper gown of a uniform colour, a long white cloth on the head, and over it a common fur cap. In the perforated right nostril they wear a ring, adorned with corals, pearls, or pre-cious stones. This is also considered as an ornament by the more elegant ladies of Astrakhan.

The Tartars lead a wandering life along the banks of the Akhtouba, from Krasnyy Yar to the vicinity of Sassikol; and are rich in flocks of sheep, but more particularly in black cattle, which they employ chiefly for drawing their chariots and baggage carts as they are not provided with camels. Their horses are numerous, but not of the best breed.

On 21st May we left the pleasant valleys and travelled over a high sandy ridge in the direction of the branch of water called Sassikol. Sassikol is a false branch of the Akhtouba, and runs to the south and south-east, in a serpentine direction, into the steppe. It consists of connected pools and bays covered with rushes, and by means of it the Akhtouba inundates the country at high water. In the month of June, when the lowest valleys are divested of their grass, and over-flowed by the Volga, the Kundure Tartars retire hither, regarding this country as the upper boundary of their pasturage. The water-sides are skirted by a pleasant low country, covered with sedge, tamarisks and willows.

A woman and girl of the Kundure Tartars in their national costume.

FROM THE SOUTHERN VOLGA TO THE CAUCASUS

MAY – AUGUST 1793

O<small>N 25TH MAY WE SET FORTH</small> for Sarepta again, where we arrived at dawn on the following day. The county of Sarepta, so advantageously situated for botanical excursions, engaged my attention so much in the month of June that I did not think of my future journey. I was, however, much against my inclination, obliged to remain here for part of July on account of the insupportable heat occasioned by the steppe, large areas of which were on fire on both sides of the Volga; and likewise from the circumstance that my daughter caught the small-pox.

Wishing, however, to undertake a journey during the fine weather, and to visit the steppe beyond the Volga, I travelled on 5th July to Tzaritzin to be ferried over the river. On the 6th I crossed the Volga, and continued my journey between that river and the Akhtouba over a low country intersected with small branches of water. The sandy and marly soil of this low country produces most excellent crops of hay. The beautiful oak trees here, as well as everywhere along the Volga, are intermixed with the *Ulmus campestris* and dwarf elms, Tartar plane trees, poplars, willows, aquatic elder trees, and other shrubs. Also are found a number of large mulberry trees bearing fruit of a white, black, and pale violet colour.

As the autumn approached I was desirous to obtain some knowledge of Mount Caucasus. On 27th August we began our journey on the road to Kizlyar. The country adjacent to the road leading to Kizlyar along the Caspian Sea is very remarkable, on account of the manifest traces of its ancient connection with the Meotic gulf of the Black Sea.

I was now obliged to continue my journey with the Turkomans, who are a wealthy, well formed and lively people. In the steppe of Kizlyar they are permitted to lead a wandering life with their flocks and herds and have a great number of camels, black cattle, sheep and horses.

Their principal food is flesh, sour milk, a small quantity of groats, and meal, which they purchase from the Russians, but their favourite food is horse flesh.

A Turkoman with his bow, quiver and whip. The Turkomans are more attached to ornamental dress than any other tribe of the steppes. They are superior in comeliness and gaiety to their brethren on the eastern shore of the Caspian Sea.

THE ROAD TO THE CAUCASUS MOUNTAINS

FROM THE LOW COUNTRY AND BAY of Alabuga, we travelled south-west over the surrounding sand-hills and descended into a region of salt lakes and pools. This extensive saline tract is succeeded by a line of drift-sand, and salt-pits, with intermediate sandy elevations. We at length arrived at a level steppe, mostly impregnated with salt, on which grew tamarisks and other marine plants. This level steppe at length declined towards a low saline country of a vast extent. We arrived in this, the Manyth, after travelling along the bank of the Sarpa on our road to the Caucasus. In the spring this low country is entirely inundated by the snow water.

The empty salt pools or fens are of the same nature as the saline lakes. In the spring and autumn they contain brackish water, but in the first fine weather of May, they entirely evaporate, and resemble the soil of a dried quagmire. Their surface is composed of a tough black mire of different degrees of thickness. They emit an effluvium like that of putrid eggs and produce no plants, except the *Salicornia herbacea*, which grows around their edge.

Since 1781 a number of new colonies have been established in the environs of the Caucasus, with an intention to people the frontiers and support the troops stationed there. Most of these villages, in consequence of disease, desertion and other causes, have lost a considerable number of their original inhabitants. At length they have now attained a permanent state of prosperity.

Further up the river Kuma are antique Tartar buildings known by the names of Bolshye or Verkhnie, or the greater or upper Madshary. The buildings that remain entire are only sepulchral mosques of a Muslim nation, perhaps of Tartar origin. There is no foundation for believing what is related of this supposed city, that its inhabitants have been expelled by great numbers of the large tarantula; notwithstanding my diligent researches, I have not been able to discover a single tarantula in those regions.

Four Tartar burial chapels or vaults of the Great Madshary. They lie in a line from east to west on the high steppe. There were apparently three principal rows, besides the sepulchral hillocks, tombstones and other ruins that are scattered around without any obvious order.

A KABARDINIAN

———————

THIS IS ONE OF THE TRIBES who are generally called Circassians (Tcherkessians). They were first subject to Russia in the 16th century. They inhabit the country in the neighbourhood of the Caucasian mountains, to the south of the Nagay Tartars, of the Sea of Azov, along the banks of the rivers Terek and Soonsha, which take their rise in the mountains near Mount Kabarda. These people at one time threw off their allegiance to Russia, massacred all the commissionaries and civil officers, and put themselves under the protection of the Turks.

The Kabardinians, as well as all the other Caucasian tribes, are stationary, and very populous. They generally live in small villages, and are employed in agriculture and pasturage, though many follow different trades and some few are engaged in commerce.

A KABARDINIAN WOMAN

THE MALE DRESS OF THIS TRIBE, as may be observed in the preceding plate, differs very little from several other tribes of Tartars; but the female dress is one of those which varies very much from that of the men, more particularly in the mode of ornamenting and embroidering it. Their head-dress is called *tastar*, and forms a veil which, when they go out, they draw over their faces. Among all the tribes comprehended in this empire red hair is considered a much greater beauty than black, at least form the women, who are in general the best made and handsomest among the Tartars. From some of these tribes come those Circassian females who grace the harem of the Grand Seignior. These are bought by Armenian merchants, and then sold to the Turks.

INTO THE CAUCASUS MOUNTAINS

AUGUST – SEPTEMBER 1793

FROM MADSHARY WE FIRST DESCRIED THE snowy mountains of the Caucasus. During the whole of a day's journey they appeared particularly distinct to us, on account of the serenity of the air, and exhibited a most magnificent spectacle. The low country abounded with a greater variety of wood than I had before observed. The wild pear, cherry, a species of small acid plums, the *Ligustrum, Evonymus grandis, Physalis Alkekengi* and *Senecio Doria* grew here in abundance: there were also numbers of pheasants, hares, and roebucks.

In the evening, we crossed the Kuma, and after travelling five versts through a bushy valley we arrived at the fortress of Georgievsk, which has since been made the chief seat of the government. It has a church; but, except the residence of the governor, there is scarcely a decent and tenantable habitation. Happily for the inhabitants, the winter is as mild here as in the mountains of the Crimea, thanks to the high mountains that protect Georgievsk against the north wind. Notwithstanding this protection, the turbid waters of the Podkuma, the sudden vicissitudes of heat and cold, especially the bleak night winds from the lofty mountains, the want of precaution in the Russian soldier to preserve himself from those nocturnal blasts, and the frequent exhalations and fogs which arise from the moist and low country, all contribute to render this place extremely unwholesome; so that intermittent and bilious fevers are endemic and very obstinate.

When we arrived at Georgievsk, the ridge of the black mountain along the Caucasus was covered with new-fallen snow, which, however, melted in a few days. From Georgievsk we had a magnificent view of the mountains, in their whole extent from the Caspian to the Black Sea.

The country in the environs of Georgievsk consists of arable land of an excellent quality, meadows, pastures, and an abundance of firewood and game: the whole tract from this place to the mountains has every requisite for the subsistence of a considerable population.

A view of the whole ridge of mountains forming part of Mount Caucasus, from the great Elburus which fronts the Black Sea to the vicinity of the Caspian, drawn in September, when part of the black mountains was already covered with fresh snow or rime.

THE HOT SPRINGS ON MOUNT METSHUKA

SEPTEMBER 1793

O N 9TH SEPTEMBER I UNDERTOOK A journey to the fortress of Constantinogorsk, which is one of the most important posts on the whole line of the Caucasus, and was built to restrain the incursions of the Circassians (Tcherkessians), Abassines and Kundure Tartars.

The villages of the Abassines in this country resemble those of the Circassians in their structure, and internal arrangement: they have, besides the necessary rooms for the family, separate apartments for visitors, and, instead of stoves, they construct chimneys of wicker-work, plastered over with clay. The roofs are slightly built of rafters, covered with herbs and long stalks of plants; the couch or sofa is a sort of divan, made of wood and placed to the left, on entering the room; it is covered with felts and bolsters. On the walls of the cabin are suspended furs and other articles of dress, arms, and variegated straw mats of exquisite workmanship. Their mode of dress also, both men and women, perfectly resemble the Circassians.

I was eager to survey the mountain Metshuka which is remarkable for the famous sulphurous bath. The mountain itself is of considerable extent, and in a conical form. Upon it we discovered many hot, sulphurous springs. The smell of sulphur, which is perceptible at a considerable distance, the snow-white tophus-stone, of a crystalline nature, and the flowers of sulphur precipitated in the channels of the descending water, are sufficient indications of the principal constituents of the water. The water itself has a sweetish taste, is hotter than the hand can bear, and evidently contains a portion of alum, which renders it serviceable in diarrhoeas and dysenteries. In rheumatic pains, cutaneous eruptions, and inveterate ulcers, it is of essential service, if used as a warm bath. Gouty and paralytic patients have recovered by its use. In intermittent fevers, however, this bath ought not to be resorted to, as it is liable to occasion dangerous obstructions.

Mount Metshuka, and the adjacent lower mountains. At a distance may be seen the summits of the Beshtau, or the mount with five heads.

THE CIRCASSIANS OF THE CAUCASUS

SEPTEMBER 1793

URING MY SHORT RESIDENCE NEAR THE mountains, I had an opportunity of collecting a variety of information relative to the inhabitants of the Caucasus, among whom are the Circassians. The branch of this nation most interesting to the historical inquirer is usually called the Great and Little Kabarda. They consider themselves as descendants of the Arabs.

The Circassians are upon the whole a handsome race of people. The men, especially among the higher classes, are mostly of a tall stature, thin form, but Herculean structure; they are very slender about the loins, have a small foot, and uncommon strength in the arms. The women are indeed not uniformly beautiful, but are for the most part well formed, have a white skin, dark brown or black hair, and regular features: I have however met with a greater number of beauties among them than in any other unpolished nation. Their females dress in a uniform style, till they are delivered of the first child, after which they begin to cover the head with a white handkerchief drawn close over the forehead and fastened below the chin. It is a custom perhaps not generally known, that their girls, between the tenth and twelfth year of their age, are provided with laced stays, or a broad girdle made of untanned leather; this singular coat of mail is among the common people tightly sewn around the waist, but in the higher classes it is fastened with silver hooks, so that they are obliged to wear it till their wedding night, when the bridegroom, with a sharp-cutting dagger, unties this gordian knot, which ceremony is frequently attended with danger.

Over the shift, the girls wear a laced jacket, because the petticoat, which reaches to the ankles, is open along the whole front, and resembles that of a man; but married women dress in wide breeches. Besides the girdle of chastity there is another circumstance which contributes to preserve the elegant shape of the girls: they are sparingly nourished, eating only a little milk and pastry.

A Circassian of distinction in his ordinary domestic dress, and a princess of that nation; in the background are Circassian houses, and natives on horseback and on foot.

THE CIRCASSIAN KNIGHT

SEPTEMBER 1793

IT IS A PRACTICE AMONG THE Circassians to compress the waist from early infancy as much as possible, by means of straps, hence they are uncommonly thin between the loins and the breast. I have also uniformly remarked that their feet are of an extraordinary small size because they force them in the tightest manner within their Morocco slippers, which gives them the appearance of dancers.

The male dress is light, neat, and becoming, and, in many respects, resembles that of the Tartars but is a more elegant shape. The upper garment is regularly furnished with a small embroidered pocket on each side of the breast for containing cartridges. On the head, which is shorn in the Polish fashion, is worn an embroidered cap quilted with cotton, in the form of a melon, but occasionally lower, and ornamented with various gold and silver laces especially among the wealthy. The whiskers are allowed to grow, as is common among the Poles.

Above the lower dress, which is made of light stuff, persons of distinction sometimes wear a short, rich waistcoat, as it were to supply the place of armour, either with or without a great- coat. The upper dress, consisting either of cloth or other strong woven stuff, is somewhat shorter than the under garment, while the sleeves are slit open, and frequently bordered with furs. The breeches are provided with knee-straps, and the seams are bound with small lace or embroidery, which the women very skilfully manufacture of gold and silver threads.

When a prince pays a visit in full dress he arrays himself with all his accoutrements and coat of arms. His helmet and arm- plates are manufactured of polished steel. In the girdle is usually carried a dagger and pistols, while the bow and quiver are tied by straps round the hips. In common visits the coat of mail is worn below the upper dress, and on such occasions the only weapon carried is a sabre.

A Circassian prince or nobleman, in full dress, with an additional jacket of mail. These coats of mail are manufactured of polished steel rings, being imported from Persia and Kubesha. The Circassian commoner is armed with a sabre and club, his constant weapons on any excursion.

THE CIRCASSIAN LAW OF REVENGE

SEPTEMBER 1793

CIRCASSIAN PRINCES AND KNIGHTS PURSUE NO other business or recreation than war, pillage, and the amusements of the chase; they live a lordly life, wander about, meet at drinking parties and undertake military excursions.

The two opposite customary laws, those of hospitality and revenge, are sacredly observed among them. He who befriends a stranger defends him not only with his own blood and life but also with that of his relatives. A stranger who entrusts himself to the patronage of a woman, or is able to touch with his mouth the breast of a wife, is spared and protected as a relation of the blood, though he were the enemy, nay even the murderer of a similar relative.

Bloody revenge, the opposite conduct, is practised with the most scrupulous adherence to custom. The murder of a family relation must be avenged by the next heir; this desire of revenge is hereditary in the successors and the whole tribe; it remains as it were rooted with so much rancour that the hostile princes or nobles of two different tribes when they meet each other on the road are compelled to fight for their lives unless they have given previous notice to each other and bound themselves to pursue a different route.

If the son or daughter of a family enter into the state of wedlock they have no right to appear before their parents during the first twelve months or till the birth of a child. During this period the husband continues secretly to visit his young wife through the window of a room but is never present when she is visited by strangers. From the earliest infancy, children are entrusted to the care of a nobleman and the parents, especially the father, have no desire to see them till they are adult: if a son, till he can bear arms, if a daughter, till after marriage. The husband generally lives in a separate apartment, and is not very fond of making his appearance before his wife.

A Circassian nobleman in his complete accoutrements and arms on horseback. In the background are Circassian dwellings.

THE INGUSHIANS OF THE CAUCASUS

SEPTEMBER 1793

THERE IS A TRIBE OF PEOPLE differing entirely from all other inhabitants of the Caucasus in language as well as in stature and countenance; their national name is Lamur; by others they are called Galgai or Ingushians. The manner of pronunciation of these semi-barbarians appeared to us as if their mouths were full of stones. We were informed that they are an honest and brave set of people, maintain their independence, and are subject only to their elders or priests by whom their religious sacrifices are performed.

They are almost the only nation inhabiting the Caucasus among whom the shield has been preserved as part of their accoutrements. These bucklers are made of wood, covered with leather, and bound with iron hoops of an oval form. The short knotty pike which forms part of their armour serves not only as a weapon of defence, but is likewise used for supporting the gun between its forked branches, by fixing the pointed end in the ground, which enables the sharpshooter to take a more accurate aim. The Ingushians are excellent marksmen but bestow little attention either to agriculture or the rearing of cattle, and are consequently in a state of poverty.

I was assured by a Roman Catholic missionary that these people possess an old church which is built according to a model taken from the sepulchre of Jesus Christ. Although it bears evident marks of antiquity it is nevertheless of so firm a construction that it only seldom requires repair. It is looked after by the Ingushians who, at present, rather incline to profess the Muslim faith. Notwithstanding this fact the church is held in such profound veneration that nobody ventures to enter it and the natives, when viewing it at a distance, prostrate themselves in adoration. In diseases, as well as on other unfortunate occasions, the church is their principal asylum.

Two Ingushians, one with his musket, apparently in a case suspended over his left shoulder, and a dagger and sabre. The other has the usual shield, and a short pike on which he rests his gun when taking aim.

COSSACKS AT TSHERKASK

ON 23RD SEPTEMBER WE LEFT GEORGIEVSK with a view to reach Taurida (the Crimea) before the setting in of the winter. We at length arrived at Stavropol where we were detained till the close of the night before we could receive the requisite number of horses for the prosecution of our journey as every person we accosted appeared to be in liquor. The intoxicated Cossacks who were our guides, instead of conducting us to the more convenient though circuitous high road, led us directly down the precipitous glen intersected by a river where we remained at least an hour before we could extricate ourselves, which fatigued the horses and occasioned considerable damage to our carriages.

We arrived at Tsherkask on 30th September. In a clear evening the northern promontory of the Caucasus may be distinctly seen from this city; the summits of the snowy mountains are also visible, glimmering and obscure, though in a direct line from thence to the river Kuban the distance is three long days' journey on horseback.

The dress of the Cossack women and girls at Tsherkask differs in every respect from that worn above the Lines of Tzaritzin. It is a complete deshabille of a peculiar kind. In their domestic employments they go barefooted, and wear trousers, which hang down as low as the ankles. When in full dress they wear slippers and stockings of yellow morocco, in the latter of which they tuck the extremities of their trousers; white linen is scarcely ever used by them except among the poor. The shifts are usually made of dyed cotton, or Asiatic silk stuffs, either of a yellow or blue colour.

We spent only one day at Tsherkask then, on 1st October, the weather again having become fair, we proceeded on our journey to Taganrog. We soon came to the new town of Nakhtshivan, the first Armenian town established in the Russian empire during the mild government of the great empress Catherine II, and one of the most promising new colonies.

A matron in the national dress of the wives of the Cossacks, and a girl, from Tsherkask.

THE PORT OF TAGANROG

WE NEXT CAME TO FORT TAGANROG on the Sea of Azov. Its market is spacious and contains numerous wooden shops; the Greeks possess a particular row of booths, where, according to the Eastern custom, they keep small taverns and coffee houses, which are chiefly frequented by sailors. Besides the principal church, within the fortress, there are two others: one for the divine service of the Russians, and another belonging to the Greeks. From the northern side of the valley, which contains the governor's house, the town commands a fine prospect. On the same side, but towards the low country contiguous to the seashore, are squares of shops, or booths, called the Exchange, where the captains of vessels, and ship owners, expose their merchandise to sale.

Next to this place is the wharf, where we noticed several merchant vessels constructed in the form of pinks, completely armed. The hospital for performing quarantine is situated to the west of the naval port, immediately below the fortress, on the open wharf.

Navigation is much interrupted here in winter, because the roads of Kertsh, and a great part of the Sea of Azov, are then covered with ice. From the mouth of the Don to the heights of Taganrog, the sea is every winter so completely frozen that travellers go in carriages upon the ice with the greatest safety. The whole shore is also to a very considerable extent covered with ice. It however often breaks in consequence of sea storms, and thus exposes the fishermen to the greatest danger. The sea generally freezes in December, and remains in that state till the month of March; but the shoals of ice in the Bosphorus delay navigation till a much later period in the spring.

Among the principal articles of exportation from Taganrog are iron, wheat, butter, tallow, ropes, sail cloth, hemp, Russian linen, slated and pressed caviar, saltpetre, leather, undressed skins, which are exported only by smugglers, bristles, hare and other furs. The Russians import wine, dried fruit, marmalade of boiled grapes, nuts, silk and cotton from Turkey, lemons, oranges and rum.

The fortress and harbour of Taganrog. In the foreground is a plantation of mulberry trees, a grove of willows, and the wharf.

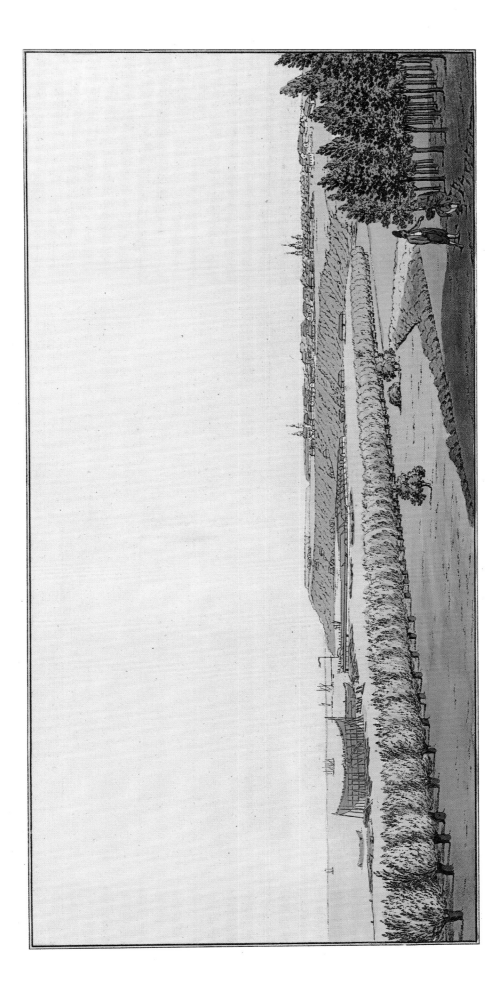

ALONG THE SHORES OF THE SEA OF AZOV

OCTOBER 1793

O N 21ST OCTOBER WE LEFT TAGANROG and crossed the river Mius. This river's valley forms an extensive basin, with steep and craggy shores, a satisfactory proof of the former existence of a bay here. We continued our journey over an elevated but level country to the river Mokroi. Beyond the river the plain became gradually more rugged, and we thus continued to the river Kalmius. We passed a few sepulchral hillocks erected of stone. On one of these sacred mounds we saw two great vultures, which are very numerous in Taurida. We crossed the river Kalmius, which is 70 fathoms broad, in a flat boat. From the ferry we proceeded along a valley to the Greek town of Mariupol. It has a good market-place, furnished with wooden booths. The houses are constructed in the Grecian style, with projecting roofs ornamented with scrolls, or brackets, and covered with hollow tiles.

Between the rivulets Berda and Moloshna we met with wandering Nagays, a very small remainder of that numerous horde which was lately distinguished by the name of Kubanian Tartars. They have only within the last two years been transferred from their former habitations in the vicinity of Kuban to these beautiful pastures where they enjoy tranquillity and abundance. The dress of the men consists of sheepskins, and a coarse kind of cloth; their caps are of different shapes, but those most generally worn are small and round, and are made of lambskins. It can be seen in the plate that the daughter's features resemble those of her father and are peculiar to the Mongol tribe, as is remarkable in most of the Nagays; her mother is of a different race. The females of this caste are not very remarkable for modesty.

A lady of distinction among the Nagays and a princess of that nation, attended by a female slave. In the background are tents constructed of felt and *arabas* or two-wheeled carts.

A FEMALE TARTAR OF THE NAGAY TRIBE

THE NAGAYS FORM ONE OF THE most considerable of the Tartar hordes; and they are the more remarkable because they have preserved, in a greater degree, most of their ancient customs and establishments; they have, however, within these few years, been much reduced both in power and numbers, and are now scattered over a great part of the Russia empire, while some of them have put themselves under the Turkish government.

The Nagays were always a pastoral nation, and inhabit that part of the empire which lies near the Sea of Azov, while another part of them live in the steppe between the Berda and Moloshnie Vody. They speak the Tartarian language, but are very illiterate. The dress of these people differs in some respects according to the place where they reside; those in the vicinity of the Sea of Azov dress differently from those on the Berda.

The females generally make their bonnets of furs, or cloth; and they wear also a sort of ornament covered with beads and pieces of money which falls down their back. Besides ornamenting their ears, they frequently bore a hole through the end of the nose, from which they suspend a gold ring, so large that it touches both their lips. The common people among the Nagays use their women very ill, and bestow but little on their dress, which is often very old and dirty, while that of the wealthy is much finer.

A MERCHANT OF KALOUGA

THE NATIVE MERCHANTS OF RUSSIA ARE included in the third division of Russian subjects, which comprehends an intermediate class of men, between the nobles and peasants. The merchants are distributed into three classes, according to the value of their capital. By the 47th article of the celebrated Manifesto of Graces, as it is called, which the late Empress Catherine conferred upon her subjects, at the conclusion of the Turkish war, in 1775, all persons who choose to enter themselves in any of the three classes are exempted from the poll tax, upon annually paying one per cent of their capital, employed in trade, to the crown.

The extent, however, of their capital is not very rigorously inquired into, for it entirely depends upon the merchants themselves to name the ostensible sum, which they are supposed to be worth; and any person possessing upwards of £2000 may, if he pleases, enrol himself in either of the inferior classes, or even in that of the burghers, if he chooses to pay the poll tax in preference to one per cent of his capital, and be entitled to no more privileges than they enjoy.

A WOMAN OF KALOUGA

KALOUGA IS THE CAPITAL TOWN OF the government of the same name, and lies within what is called the "middle region" of Russia. The state of agriculture in this district is not very good, and the produce of the land is barely equal to supply the wants of the year. There are considerable iron works, and the forests, with which it abounds, facilitate the working of them. The iron made here is exported by river. At Kalouga there are also several manufactories of linen and wool, of sail-cloth, silk, sugar, paper, tanning and distilling, but the principal trade consists in hemp, hemp oil, corn, tallow and cattle.

MERCHANT'S WIFE OF KALOUGA

THE PRECEDING PLATE SHOWED A MERCHANT'S wife in her summer dress, and opposite is shown her winter attire. These dresses are of a singular but brilliant appearance, particularly the head-dress, being embroidered and highly ornamented. The only difference between the summer and winter habits seems to be the addition of a sort of handkerchief to the head, and a cloth coat or cloak trimmed with fur thrown over the shoulders.

SECTION II

THE CRIMEAN PENINSULA

BY THE TIME THAT PROFESSOR PALLAS embarked on his journey through the Crimea, the region had become a popular tourist area. European travellers loved it: here were all the ingredients of a *Picaresque* landscape – rugged mountains, beautiful valleys watered by mountain streams, wild flowers, a dramatic coastline, fertile vine-planted slopes, and an almost perfect climate.

Professor Pallas was by no means immune to the charms of the Crimea, and his writings abound with descriptions of the mountains, the Black Sea coast, the acres of wild flowers stretching to a horizon that coloured whole vistas blue, red, yellow or white. But he is also interested in the peoples of the region and in how it is faring as part of the Russian empire.

He starts his journey at Perekop, an important and lively town that forms the gateway from the Black Sea into Russia. He and his family pass the winter at Sympheropol and then, in March 1794, begin their exploration of the peninsula.

Pallas first describes the Tartar town of Bakhtshisarai, with its mosques and khan's palace. There is a strong Turkish flavour about this "ancient seat of the Tartar khans"; to us the crooked, mean, ir-regular streets, the domes of the mosques and the steep orchards be-tween the houses may seem highly picturesque, though perhaps they were less so to Professor Pallas.

Sevastopol was the next important town on Pallas's route, and although its situation is very beautiful it seems to him a dull town, predominantly a port and naval base. The surrounding countryside, however, is full of fascination, with classical ruins scattered every-where on the coastal hilltops. He pauses at Inkerman – the site of a savage battle during the Crimean War, some 60 years later – to in-vestigate some curious monastic cells carved into the rock-face, before the next stage of his journey: the exploration of the Crimean mountains.

These mountains rise almost straight up out of the sea, and are responsible for great local variations in climate. Pallas, like other travellers of the time, often associated the climate of a particular place with its reputation as a healthy or unhealthy spot. "Fogs and vapours" were thought to be a common cause of ill-health, so the "air" of a town, a valley, or a mountainous region would often be blamed for attacks of fever or other little-understood disorders.

Pallas passes Balaklava and then travels along the south coast of the Crimea to reach the beautiful valley of Simaus, where olives, pomegranates, figs, vines and other fruits flourish in the hot climate. From there he travels to Yalta and then Karassubasar, another Moorish town that, again, Pallas admits is charming – when viewed from a distance.

Pallas then begins a fascinating account of the Tartars, natives of the Crimea, whom he feels are "on the whole ... at present un-profitable and unworthy inhabitants of those paradisiacal valleys in which they have always shown themselves the first and most ready to revolt against the Russian government." He continues disapprov-ingly: "To sit with a pipe in their hands, frequently without smok-ing, for many hours on a shady bank or hill though totally devoid of all taste for the beauties of nature ... or, if at work, to make long pauses and above all to do nothing, constitute their supreme enjoy-ments." He is especially and coldly critical of the education of Tartar boys, which takes place in the harems.

In July 1794, Professor Pallas considers that his exploration of the Crimean peninsula is completed and sets out on the return journey to St Petersburg.

South-Western Russia
and the Crimea

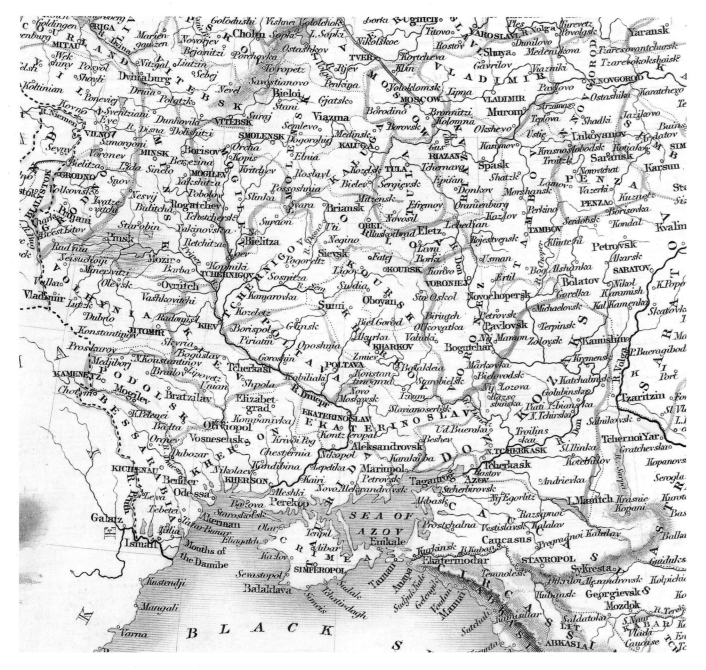

A detail from a map of Europe in Russia taken from *The Illustrated Atlas of the Nineteenth-Century World* edited by Montgomery Martin and first published in 1851.

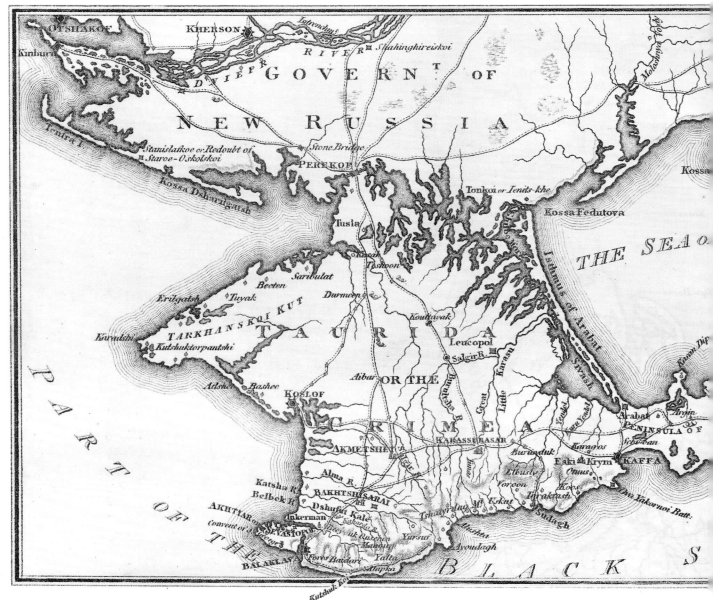

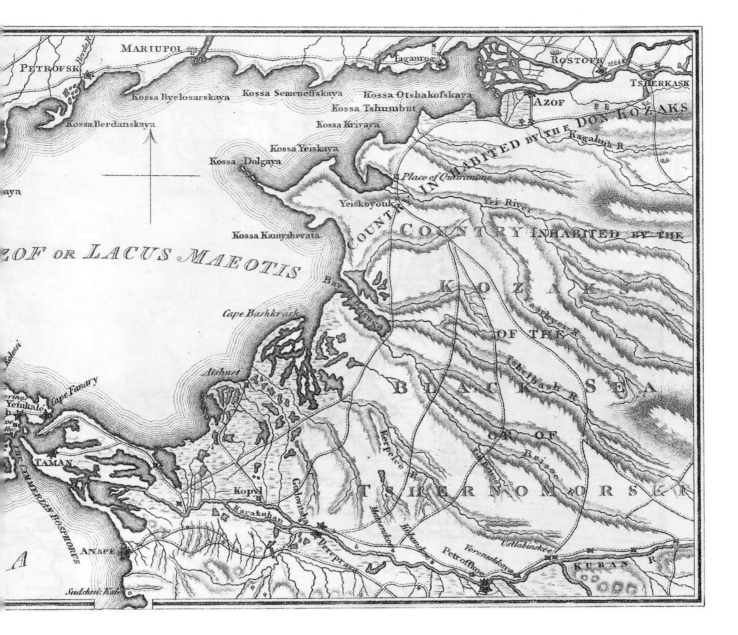

PETROFSK

MARIUPOL

Kossa Berdanskaya

Kossa Byelosarskaya

Kossa Semenofiskaya

Kossa Tshumbut

Kossa Krivaya

Kossa Yeiskaya

Kossa Dolgaya

Taganrog

ROSTOFF

TSHERKASK

Azof

COUNTRY INHABITED BY THE DON KOZAKS

Ragalnik R.

Place of Quarantine

Yei River

Yeiskoyouk

Kossa Kamyshevata

COUNTRY INHABITED BY THE

OF OR LACUS MAEOTIS

Vassilyei R.

KOZAKS

OF THE

Cape Bashkrach

Tshelbash R.

BLACK SEA

Atshuet

OF

Cape Fanary

Yenikale

Beisoo

Kerpelze R.

TAMAN

THE CIMMERIAN BOSPHORUS

Kopyl

Karakuban

Beepran

Montastoo

Tshernomorska

Malancheoy

Petrofskoe

Voronezhkaya

Ustlabinskoe

KUBAN R.

ANAPE

Sudshuk Kal.

A

THE GATE TO THE CRIMEA

1793

AS THE WHOLE CRIMEAN PENINSULA IS connected with the continent only by the isthmus of Perekop it is highly probable that the Crimea anciently, with its more elevated southern part, formed a complete island when the waters of the Black Sea were also higher, as appears from various historical passages of the ancients. Indeed, the only entrance into the Crimea by land is over a bridge, and through an arched stone gate, both erected at the side of the fortress. Contiguous to the gate, in an eastern direction and within the precincts of the fosse, is situated the fortress of Perekop, a model of irregular fortification, which together with the walls of its deep ditch, is constructed wholly of freestone.

Although the Crimea is at present united to Russia, Perekop will, on many accounts, always remain a post of the greatest consequence, in some respects to Russia, and in others to the Crimea. If, for instance, the plague should ever spread its baneful influence into Crim-Tartary, an event which the constant trade carried on with Constantinople and Anatolia might easily produce, or if seditious commotions should arise among the Tartars, whose loyalty is still doubtful, in these cases Perekop would effectually secure the empire by closely shutting the barrier.

On the other hand, this fortress renders every attempt at desertions from the Crimea into Russia very difficult. Further, if the best ports of the Crimea were appointed in the same manner as those of Toulon and Marseille have been selected for all the southern parts of France, in order to establish places of quarantine for all ships navigating the Black Sea and the Sea of Azov, the important pass of Perekop would for ever secure the open and more populous provinces of the interior parts of the empire from that terrible scourge, the plague. Thus all danger might be obviated not only from the Sea of Azov, the coasts of which are in every direction exposed to the contagion so that they can only with difficulty be protected, but also from the ports of Kherson, Nikolayev and Odessa.

The gate of Perekop, which presents a lively, bustling scene throughout the summer. In the foreground are carts from Russia Minor, laden with grain, which will take back salt from the Crimea; travelling carriages; and Tartar waggons drawn by camels or horses.

PEREKOP TO SYMPHEROPOL

WINTER 1793 – 4

THE NORTHERN THREE QUARTERS OF THE Crimean peninsula exhibit an irregular plain or steppe, which is occasionally diversified with deeper spots of ground, or hollow glens. The inexhaustible reservoirs of salt in the vicinity of Perekop are the most productive of the whole peninsula.

Early on 30th October we arrived at Sympheropol (or Akmetshet, its Tartar name) and were taken to the winter residence that had been prepared for my family. Nothing can be conceived more gratifying, after an irksome journey over barren and uniform plains, than a view of mountains, and a country presenting hills and beautifully variegated woods occasionally intersected by the whimsical meanders of rivulets.

The fine and often very warm weather which prevailed during the whole of November afforded me frequent opportunities of collecting, at this late season, the seeds of several rare plants. On 27th November, at half past eight in the evening, we perceived the slight shock of an earthquake which was also felt at Perekop, but which was incomparably milder than that which convulsed the whole southern coast of this peninsula in 1790.

In the beginning of March the weather became so agreeable that I could no longer restrain my impatience to explore the remarkable Tauridan peninsula. I left Sympheropol on the 8th of the month and directed my course towards Bakhtshisarai. The town occupies a narrow dale, being enclosed on both sides with high rocky terraces. The streets are built on a gradual ascent above each other, very crooked, narrow, mean, irregular, and in a most filthy state, but prettily interspersed with orchards. These in turn are interspersed with Lombardy poplars, which, together with the numerous turrets of the mosques and the handsome chimneys of dwelling houses, that are in other respects mostly in a wretched condition, afford pleasing views of this ancient town.

Bakhtshisarai, the ancient residence of the Tartar khan. The palace of the khan, the mosques, the sepulchral monuments of the khans, and the castle garden, set among gardens and trees, make an agreeable picture.

BAKHTSHISARAI: A TARTAR TOWN

MARCH 1794

THE PRINCIPAL EMBELLISHMENTS OF BAKHTSHISARAI are its mosques, or *metshets*, its school houses, its baths, and the khan's palace. There are 31 mosques in the town, well built and surrounded with lofty towers of elegant workmanship. There are 21 taverns, 17 Tartar coffee houses, and 517 shops selling silks, shoes and other leather articles, groceries, Tartar knives and other cutlery manufactured in great perfection, silver articles, rope, wool, earthenware and candles.

The khan's palace deserves particular notice. It is situated towards the western quarter of the town, and consists of various dwellings and offices built without any order, and encompassing several courtyards. The apartments and galleries above-stairs are decorated totally after the Turkish manner, with carpets and divans, oriental landscapes, clumsy paintings on the walls, artificial flowers, chimney-pieces and stained glass windows. The alterations we noticed in some of these apartments were made for the reception of the Empress in 1787 in order to embellish them more in the European style. Amidst the dwellings appropriated to the Khan there is a beautiful oblong spot planted with rose trees and ornamented with arbours, above which a fountain plays its waters into stone basins gradually declining a few steps beneath the surface of the ground.

The grand mosque in front of the palace is a most elegant temple. In the interior there is a kind of box furnished with windows, formerly appropriated to the family of the khan. At present only strangers, and particularly females, are admitted to this box, to witness the religious ceremonies of the Tartars, especially the noisy and whimsical dances of their dervishes on Fridays or on the evenings of their festivals.

Immediately below the town are those ancient sepulchral vaults of the khans called by the Tartars Eski Yourt, or the Old Habitations. The modern rage for desolation has also extended itself to these respectable monuments of antiquity, and unprincipled persons have profaned this sanctuary of the dead, broken out the ornaments, and basely converted them into chimney pieces.

Eski Yourt, the ancient Tartar sepulchral monuments, near the village of the same name. The latest and most beautiful is vaulted in the form of a cupola. Its doors and windows were once framed with cornices of white marble, but this has sadly been stolen.

AN OSTIAK OF THE OBE

BEFORE THE RUSSIANS CONQUERED SIBERIA, IT was under the dominion of the Tartars, who gave the name of Ouschtaik, signifying savage, to the nations who inhabit it, as a mark of their contempt; hence they were called Ostiaki. The Ostiaks are divided into two branches; those who live in the vicinity of the river Obe, and those who are established about Obdor and Berezov. The Ostiaki are the most numerous nations of Siberia, where the population, on account of the rigour of the climate, is not very great. These people seldom exceed the middle size, and are not remarkable for their beauty; their complexion is yellowish, and their hair generally a deep red, yet they are not ill made. They are in a state of great barbarism, and get their living chiefly by hunting and fishing, as none of them cultivate the soil.

They have neither horses, beasts, nor sheep; their livestock consists of reindeer, of which some have more than 200. Their dress is generally formed of the skins of different animals and furs. They wear short trousers; their stockings are made of skin, which go all over the feet, and serve them for boots; which they strengthen by placing the skin double for the sole. They have a sort of jacket next their skin, and over all they put a long coat, with close sleeves, which has a hood which entirely covers their head, and only leaves out the face; and in very cold weather they even wear another over this.

AN OSTIAK IN WINTER HUNTING DRESS

THIS NATION, ESPECIALLY THAT PART WHICH inhabits the neighbour-hood of the river Obe, divide their time between fishing and hunting, the latter occupying the winter months. Their skill, however, is greater in fishing than in hunting. They frequently go out in parties of ten or twelve persons, and remain in the deserts for six weeks together, taking their provisions with them, consisting chiefly of dried fish, which they draw after them on sledges; some-times, indeed, they make their dogs, which they also use in hunting, draw them. The bow is most general, though firearms are also used.

For the purpose of travelling over the snow, they fasten a large piece of board to their feet, not unlike a canoe in shape. Their prin-cipal food is fish, which they preserve, by drying, for their winter use. Instead of bread, they use fish, dried in the air, and then beaten into powder.

A FEMALE OSTIAK

THE WOMEN, IN SUMMER, WEAR THE same sort of dress as the men, which is all made from the skins of fish; but over this they wear in winter a long loose gown or coat, made sometimes of tanned leather, and sometimes of cloth, or fur from the reindeer. They cover their head with a sort of hood or veil, which falls down to their shoulders, but which, when they work, they lift up; it is always either bordered or fringed all round. The employment of the females consists in drying fish, from the entrails of which they procure oil; they also prepare a kind of glue from them, and tan the skin.

The Ostiaks, both male and female, are addicted to drunkenness; but, as they have little else to drink besides water, they contrive to intoxicate themselves with the fumes of tobacco, and by eating a species of mushroom. When intoxicated, they become extravagantly gay, they sing and jump and make a noise; but, on their return to their senses, after taking some sleep, they seem to have forgotten everything that has passed.

THE PORT OF SEVASTOPOL

MARCH 1794

THE HARBOUR OF SEVASTOPOL IS AT present called Akhtiar, or Ak-Yar, from a Tartar village formerly situated on the north side of the harbour, three versts from Inkerman. On account of its excellent port the building of this place was commenced immediately after the occupation of the Crimea and has since very rapidly increased. The supply of provisions from the adjacent villages is very deficient on account of the apprehensions which the Tartars entertain of the sailors, so that every article is sold at an extravagant price.

There is a worse abuse practised at Sevastopol which requires an immediate remedy: the petty dealers in this place, being mostly Greeks, are not contented with moderate profits, but greatly oppress the subaltern naval officers and seamen, not only by the arbitrary and exorbitant rates of their goods, but also by illicit modes of discounting bank notes and Turkish silver currency. Instances have sometimes occurred in which sailors have been paid in paper money that bore a discount of from 10 to 12 per cent which they were obliged to exchange for copper coin. Further, Turkish currency, that formerly abounded in the Crimea, was by the same usurers reduced to 15 per cent lower than its usual value, and besides, the prices of all merchandize were advanced. This unprincipled conduct, which surpasses even that of Jews, has often been carried to such extent that the mariners have nearly been induced to commit riots and other excesses.

At present, Russian dealers purchase cattle on the steppe, and drive them to market; but formerly butcher's meat was sold cheaper by mariners, who then enjoyed more liberty, and often resorted to illicit methods of procuring it. Their common slaughtering places were in thickets, on the mountains of Inkerman, whence the meat was conveniently sent to town. This illegal spot was generally known from the large brown vultures hovering around it in circular flights.

The port and town of Sevastopol, with a flotilla lying at anchor in the roads. On the most remote point can be seen the ruins of the ancient Chersonesus.

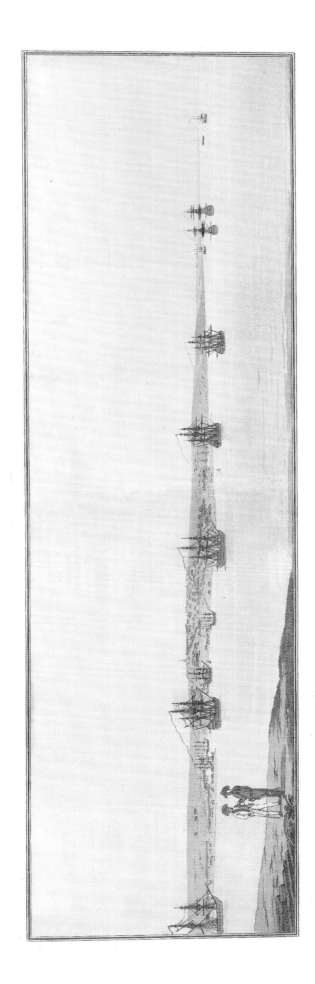

CLASSICAL REMAINS AT INKERMAN

MARCH 1794

THE ENVIRONS OF SEVASTOPOL MAY BE considered as truly classic ground on almost every step of which the enquirer meets with Greek antiquities that must have been still more numerous before the town of Sevastopol had risen from the ruins of the ancient Chersonesus (Cherronesus).

This city flourished in the time of Strabo. When the Crimea became a Russian province there still remained the greater part of the wall built of handsome freestone, as well as of the fine gate leading to the city, and a considerable portion of two strong towers, but the rise of Sevastopol has completed the ruin of the ancient city. Modern builders, careless about the gigantic plans and noble designs of their ancestors, have removed those handsome square stones from the very foundations, and employed them in erecting new houses without showing the slightest curiosity for drawing a single view or architectural sketch. What does appear from fragments of Latin inscriptions is that this place was formerly in the possession of the Genoese. Copper and silver medals, and some of gold, coined in the reigns of Gordian, Aurelian, Constantius, even that of Augustus, are found here. Fragments of white and blue enamel of different shades, and of common glass, are also found.

A remarkable specimen of antiquity is the old fortress of Inkerman, erected at the extreme point of the harbour of Sevastopol, together with the neighbouring caverns. These caverns have, in my opinion, been excavated by Arian monks during the reigns of the Greek emperors in the middle or later ages when they were severely persecuted and fled to Korssun. Unable to procure an asylum in this city they began to form cells and construct chapels in the soft calcareous rock, both here and in many parts of Crim-Tartary, where they peaceably followed a monastic life, possibly with the hope of converting the savage inhabitants. Some of the rock is so completely excavated that its open cells resemble the form of beehives, and the walls are frequently less than a hand's span in thickness.

The monastic cells at Inkerman, hewn out of the rock. The fortified wall that defended the ancient fortress of Inkerman, which belonged first to the Greeks, then to the Genoese, can also be seen.

INKERMAN TO TSHORGUNA

MARCH 1794

THE LAST OBJECT WORTHY OF NOTICE is the Greek monastery of Saint George. It is situated in a slight excavation of the southern, rocky, and very high shore of the Chersonesus, between the terrific promontory of Aya-Burun and the prominent corner of a rock called Georgievskoi Muis, or Cape George. From the uppermost and uniformly rocky terrace of this prominence the shore declines with alternate steep elevations to the level of the sea, so that the highest narrow terraces have been adapted to dwellings and those in the lower parts have been converted into vineyards.

The rocks supporting the upper terrace impend so remarkably over the church and convent that the slightest earthquake would occasion their downfall. Beneath these precipices occur several grottos, some of which are inhabited by monks, while others are employed as poultry houses. The situation of the convent is uncommonly warm, being directly exposed to the meridian sun and secured from all the cold winds, but during tempests from the south and south-west it presents terrific scenes. The monastery consists of a small church, a spacious refectory connected with it by covered passages, and some tolerable apartments which are inhabited by a few Greek monks. The place is celebrated for the parties of pleasure and the pilgrimages that are undertaken on Saint George's day in April, principally by the Greek families throughout the Crimea.

I was anxious to avail myself of the fine spring weather and on Easter Sunday I departed with my wife and daughter, quitting the western post road leading to Sevastopol and proceeding in a direct line towards the south-west on the imperial road by which the Empress visited Sevastopol, Balaklava and the celebrated valley of Vaidari. We began to ascend the lofty calcareous mountain, on the northern side of which the large-flowered *Orimula uniflora* was in blossom and uncommonly abundant, bearing in general white, less frequently pale yellow, and more rarely pale violet flowers. The beautiful Crimean Wood Peony, or *Paeonia triternata*, was in full vigour.

The Greek monastery of Saint George, with the gardens and vineyards in terraces on the rising coast. In the distance is the Cape of Balaklava.

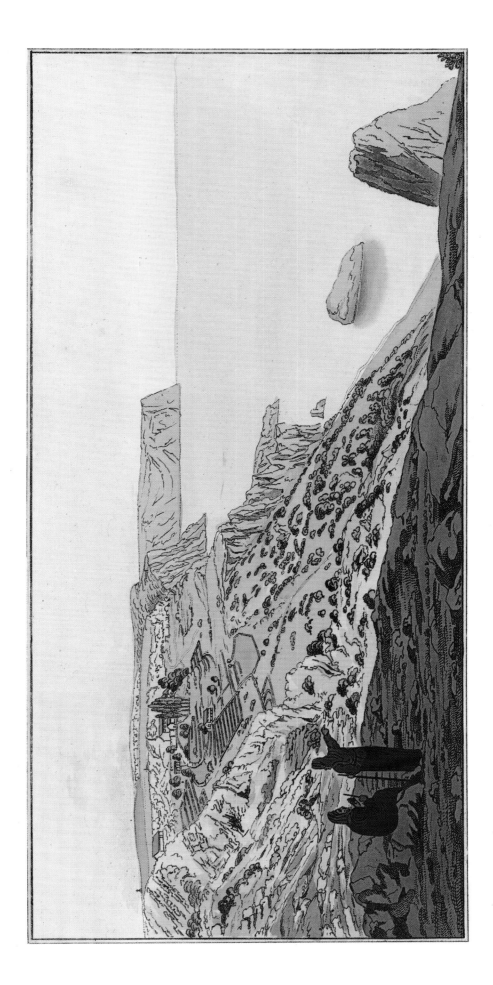

A VOTIAKIAN WOMAN

THE VOTIAKI INHABIT THE GOVERNMENTS OF Kazan and Viatka, together with some neighbouring districts. Their population is considerable, and their chief employment is agriculture. They are in general honest, hospitable and peaceable, but very superstitious. In their manners they approach nearer to the Finns than any other nation, who derive their origin from the last; yet their language is peculiar to themselves. They are ignorant of the use of writing, and instead of their signatures they make use of certain marks. They do not count by years, but months, which they name after some natural event. They live entirely to themselves, and suffer no other people to intermix, or live, with them. The women are of a timid and modest character, yet diligent and laborious. They employ themselves in spinning, making linen and cloth; they both make and embroider their own clothes.

Their dress is very singular and striking: they wear a shift, worked round the border and down the sleeves, which they fasten by a girdle so that a part of it is drawn together in front and behind. In winter they wear a large robe over it, with open sleeves, very much worked and embroidered, and of a bright colour. Their head-dress is formed of linen, folded into a certain shape, much ornamented, and fringed all round. They support it at some height from the head by means of an elastic substance, and the ends fall down upon their shoulders. Besides all this, which has a very singular appearance, they wear earrings and bracelets, made of yellow copper, brass or iron. This nation always purchase their wives, and although such as are still heathens may have as many as they like, they generally confine themselves to one.

A BASHKIRIAN WOMAN

THE BASHKIRS ARE SO CALLED FROM their great attention to the cultivation of bees. They inhabit the country in the vicinity of the southern Ural mountains, and part of the government of Oufa. They reside for the most part in villages, and their language, manners, and customs are similar to the Tartars of Kazan. During the summer months they generally lead a wandering life, always moving, with their tents and cattle, from place to place; but in the winter they confine themselves to their villages.

The women resemble those of Kazan in their dress, except in some variation in the ornaments. Instead of common tea, they make an infusion of a reddish root, which they drink without milk; it is very astringent, or the flavour would not be unpalatable. The ceremonies of their marriage are similar to the Tartars of Kazan. These people have a custom of burying their dead near some forest, and they generally make a sort of wooden hut by way of tomb, which, from being of a similar form to those they live in, appear at a little distance like their villages.

EASTER IN THE CRIMEAN MOUNTAINS

MARCH 1794

WE PASSED THE EASTER HOLIDAYS AT the village of Tshernaya Derevna, its Russian name, or Tshorguna. Under the friendly roof of Privy Counsellor Hablitzl the agreeable days that I have enjoyed at this hospitable place will never be obliterated from my memory; it has repeatedly afforded me asylum for repose after my excursions to the western mountains of the Crimea and also served as a point of reunion with my relations.

I would like to give a description of the mountains of the Crimea. The oldest and most lofty mountains of Taurida form the southern, and in a manner abrupt, border of this beautiful peninsula. They extend from Balaklava to the vicinity of Theodosia, or Kaffa, a length of nearly 150 versts. They consist of high ridges and crests, and are remarkably divided by broad and narrow valleys, craggy on the south side, which is diversified with rocky terraces, but more gradually declining towards the north. Along the sea coast the mountains present an almost uninterrupted chain of prodigious lofty precipices, declining in a northerly direction towards the steep calcareous inland rocks, and forming those bleak and elevated alpine flats which the Tartars denominate yaila, and preferably visit during hot summers on account of the rich pastures they afford for cattle, though such tracts are covered with snow till the latter end of May.

At the sea coast the Crimean mountains are so high and steep that in several places, a few versts only from the shore, they rise to a height of 1000 feet and upwards above the level of the Black Sea; according to the observations of mariners their bed or base is, for the most part, said to be similarly steep and of a depth perhaps exceeding their height, because no ground can be discovered by the plummet at a distance of one verst from the coast. The soft places for casting anchor are chiefly around the promontories, but towards the rocky bays the whole abounds with shelves by which the cable is apt to be cut and materially injured.

The valley and village of Tshorguna affords one of the most beautiful prospects in Crim-Tartary. In this plate can be seen a Turkish dwelling house, and a Tartar shepherd, and in the background are the mountains that enclose the valley of Baidari.

THE HARBOUR OF BALAKLAVA

APRIL 1794

THE ANCIENT FORTRESS OF BALAKLAVA WAS probably erected by the Greeks, and subsequently repaired by the Genoese, though it is now in a ruinous and deserted condition. The town itself has probably received its modern name from the strong Greek castle of Pallakium. It was formerly inhabited by Tartars, but as most of the natives emigrated, or were dispersed, when the Crimea was occupied by the Russians this town together with the surrounding country was granted to a regiment of Albanians, now reduced to one battalion. Thus Balaklava has been completely changed into a Greek town.

The town is close to the harbour, along the foot of the mountain, but it is not provided with good water. As the port is deep, sheltered by high mountains and narrow towards the sea, its waters are in general as calm as those of a pond, so that fishing in them is very seldom interrupted. There are mackerels and red sea mullet, which is one of the most delicate fish caught in the lakes of this country, whether it be eaten in a fresh or pickled state. Mackerels also become as tender and savoury as herrings, after being kept twelve months in brine.

The length of the harbour does not exceed one verst and a half, and its breadth is about 200 fathoms. The entrance is very deep, yet being confined within high rocks its channel scarcely admits two vessels to sail abreast. Notwithstanding the apparent danger in entering this port, it afforded a salutary refuge to such vessels as were driven by storms against the Crimean peninsula. As, however, smuggling could not be easily prevented on account of the confined situation of the harbour, the government was at length induced, in 1796, to prohibit all ships whatever from entering it, because the mercenary Greeks readily encouraged illicit traffic, so as continually to expose this neighbourhood to infection from the plague. In consequence of such exclusion several shipwrecks have already been occasioned.

Balaklava from the western extremity of the harbour, showing the old fortress erected on inaccessible rocks close to the mouth of the harbour and fortified with high walls and towers.

ALONG THE CRIMEAN COAST

APRIL 1794

THE REGIMENT OF ARNAUTES IS NOT incorporated with those of the line; it was raised chiefly of Greeks who had been in the Russian service in the Archipelago. For their support the Imperial Court not only granted the territory of Balaklava and its surrounding country and villages, but also allowed them pay and provisions. During peace, however, they seldom perform duty, because a small number only is required to be on guard, or as patrols against occasional depredations, and at present they are also obliged to form piquets for the security of the southern coast.

Few of these fencibles cultivate either vineyards or fields, and still fewer employ themselves in fishing, for which they have excellent opportunities. Their principal occupation is that of keeping petty shops in the towns of Crim-Tartary, where they are dispersed as leave of absence is readily obtained.

From Balaklava my next route was directed along the southern coast of the Crimea. I commenced this journey on horseback on 4th April when the peach, almond, apricot and plum trees were flowering in the gardens, while in the woods the *Prunus spinosa*, *Berberis vulgaris*, and the *Lantana* were only just beginning to show their blossoms.

The next day we passed through the village of Kutshuk-koi where, on 10th February 1786, the surface of the earth around the deep glens here, and in another still further eastward, began to burst, and to show rents or clefts, so that the brook which had hitherto turned two small mills constructed by the native Tartars entirely disappeared.

Two days after, the soil having become detached, and the frightened inhabitants of the adjacent village having removed their cattle, carried off their effects and abandoned their homes, the whole tract between the hollows, from the lofty bank of rocks to the seashore, fell in about midnight with a dreadful noise, and this sinking continued until 28th February, so as to produce a terrifying abyss from 10 to 20 fathoms deep, in which only a large parallel ridge of hard rock and two smaller crests remained projecting at the bottom.

A common Arnaute with his wife in ordinary dress.

THE PARADISIAC VALLEY OF SIMAUS

APRIL 1794

Eighteen versts further along the coast we reached the village of Simaus situated in a delightful valley, where a number of old olive trees occasionally disposed in rows, and numerous pomegranate trees, are interspersed between excellent orchards.

The valley of Simaus is enclosed on its eastern side by a promontory called Crotis Burun, from which we enjoyed a prospect over the dale that was peculiarly charming. Behind this eastern cape we had a view of the lofty mountains that surround the remarkably warm valley of Alupka with uninterrupted banks of steep craggy rocks, and this promontory, being the most southerly part of the ridge, is probably the Ram's Head of the ancient Greek navigators. On arriving at the top of Crotis Burun, we could completely survey the enclosed valley of Alupka, and we distinctly perceived the warm air thence wafted to us, even in the cold weather of spring. The village of Alupka itself lies on the banks of a large brook that flows in steep cascades down the steep mountains, and with all its houses and gardens and some of its arable land, is situated upon and between prodigious fragments of rock fallen towards the sea from a lofty bank.

In the mountainous parts of this region forests of pine trees are frequently met with, but their tops are mostly bent or inflected, except in low grounds, where the stems grow erect. The Tartars, however, exert their utmost endeavours to eradicate such useful species of wood by depriving it of its resin, setting fire to it, and by similar destructive means. The resin extracted from this tree affords an agreeable fumigation, not inferior to that of the mountain pine.

All the productions of the East requiring a hot climate would prosper here. Fig, pomegranate and olive trees, beside those planted in gardens, grow abundantly between the rocks in a native state, while the laurel tree, every species of wild fruit tree, vines, the *Diospyros, Terebinthus,* and *Celtis* are most common. A few cypress trees, the *Laurocerasus, Mimosa arborea,* the box tree, and other plants introduced from Constantinople are in a thriving condition.

The valley of Simaus, on the southern coast, with its abundant olive trees. This dale commands an open view of the Black Sea, and gives an idea of the beauty of this part of the Crimea.

A KIRGHI ON HORSEBACK

THE HORDES OF THE KIRGHIS ARE very well known, but never mentioned with respect, as their chief employment is robbery and plunder. They are divided into three hordes, of which only the two smaller ones are under the Russian government. These inhabit the country lying between the rivers Ural and Embo; they lead, however, a very wandering life, and frequently extend their predatory excursions along the Volga and the shores of the Caspian Sea.

The manners and appearance of these people are very striking: their countenance like most other Tartar tribes is open; their look is animated, though their eyes are small. They have long been noted for their love of plunder, and cruel adventures; but this disposition is perhaps more owing to their mode of life, and the false ideas they have of courage and glory, than to any inherent cruelty and ferociousness. They never possess any fixed habitation, but live in portable tents; consequently, their means of existence, independent of plunder, consist of their herds and flocks. In order to prevent their depredations, the Russian government have established a great number of different military posts on their frontiers.

A FEMALE KIRGHI

IT IS SAID THAT THESE HORDES rather improve both in their conduct and civilization, and this is in a great measure to be attributed to their women, who are not only prudent and good managers, but possess also a feeling and compassionate disposition, which they particularly show towards those slaves whom their husbands bring home from their predatory excursions. They have often been known to favour their escape, even when in danger of ill treatment from their husbands on that account. The employment of the women consists in taking care of the cattle, tanning the skins, making woollen cloth, etc. The men dress in a similar way to other Tartars, and the women not unlike those of Kazan, and the former also pay as much attention to the furniture of their horses as they do to their own dress.

Of these different dresses the pictures themselves afford the best descriptions. The Kirghis have the character of being most enormous eaters; their greatest delight is to devour large quantities of fat and butter without any bread. Like all other Tartars every individual of these tribes smokes tobacco to a great excess, and also takes it in powder; and they prefer the most common sort because it soonest affects the head.

YALTA AND KARASSUBASAR

APRIL – MAY 1794

THE ROAD FROM ALUPKA TO YALTA, a distance of 14 versts, leads first through a large and deep circular valley, watered by the brook Karakunda and embellished with orchards and particularly with olive trees. The next valley is intersected by the rapid brook Hastagaya, or the Painful Stream, so called because of the floods that frequently carry off cattle and dash them with fatal violence against the rocks.

The land all along this coast and its environs was, in former times, almost exclusively peopled by Greeks. Yalta, itself an ancient Greek colony, is at present inhabited only by a few Tartar families. It lies contiguous to the sea on a lofty cape which is intersected by a rivulet bearing the same name. Its Greek church was accidentally blown up by gunpowder in one of the late Turkish wars. The environs of Yalta are adapted to the culture of all such fruits and vegetables as require a warm soil and climate. The surrounding mountains are amply provided with the *Pinus maritima* and other trees.

Our route on towards the south-eastern mountains of the Crimea took us over heights and rocky promontories of spectacular and terrifying formation, interspersed with dales laid out with orchards, gardens and vineyards.

During the month of May I made several excursions over the mountain Tshatyrdag, which when viewed from the plain country is the highest mount in the Crimea, and spent a considerable time in examining the minerals, fossils and plants that are to be found all along this beautiful and mountainous country. One of my expeditions took me to the town of Karassubasar, which is in itself a place of mean appearance, and its streets are filthy beyond description. On account of the adjacent mountains the place is excessively hot in the summer, and there is a great want of drinking water, yet the inhabitants are not, in any remarkable degree, exposed to diseases, though we observed among them few persons of a healthy complexion.

The eastern part of Karassubasar, which is enlivened by the magnificent Tash-khan, one of the main mercantile halls, several mosques, and a garden surrounded with numerous poplar trees. In the foreground appears a manufactory of tiles.

MOUNTAINS OF SOUTH-EASTERN CRIMEA

MAY 1794

THE PRINCIPAL SOUTH-EASTERN MOUNTAINS OF the Crimea deserve separate notice, on account of their individual peculiarities. Of the whole chain, Mount Kushkaya, in the plate behind the fortress of Sudagh, is the first that becomes covered with moist clouds wafted from the sea, and which frequently arise during serene summer days, but more commonly in the spring and autumn; they also speedily envelop the summit of the Pertshamkaya. When these vapours settle around the eastern lofty hill Golaya and descend into the valley they are in such case mostly succeeded by rain.

Although the mountains in general that surround the dale of Sudagh are not among the highest of Taurida, they are uncommonly dissevered, steep, and therefore at first sight considerably larger than they would appear if they had more gradual slopes. They present an assemblage of various minerals, in consequence of which the hills exhibit diversified figures. This valley is, on its eastern side, contracted by a barren, round, lofty hill termed Altshak-kaya, and forming cliffs within the sea; it consists of the marmoraceous limestone which the Tartars uniformly denominate Kokatsh, or the Blue Rock; on the western side the vale is bounded not only by a still higher conoidal mount, the aforementioned Kushkaya, or Eagle's Rock, composed of a similar fossil, and being covered with pine trees on its more gradual northern declivity, while every part exposed to the sea is inaccessible; but likewise by another rock that is separated from the preceding by a deep narrow glen; has also a steep verge towards the sea; and on the summit of which is situated the ancient Genoese fortress of Sudagh.

On withdrawing from the shore farther into the country, we observed on both sides of the valley extensive mountains partly wooded. Towards the north the proper vineyard grounds of the vale are confined by a moderate ridge known by the name of Gridatly which has the form of a crescent, is composed of alternate layers of breccia and sand stone and by intercepting the sun's rays greatly contributes to improve the grapes raised in this lower tract.

The ancient Genoese fortress of Sudagh and the Kushkaya mountain which lies behind it, giving an idea of this form of mountain in the Crimea.

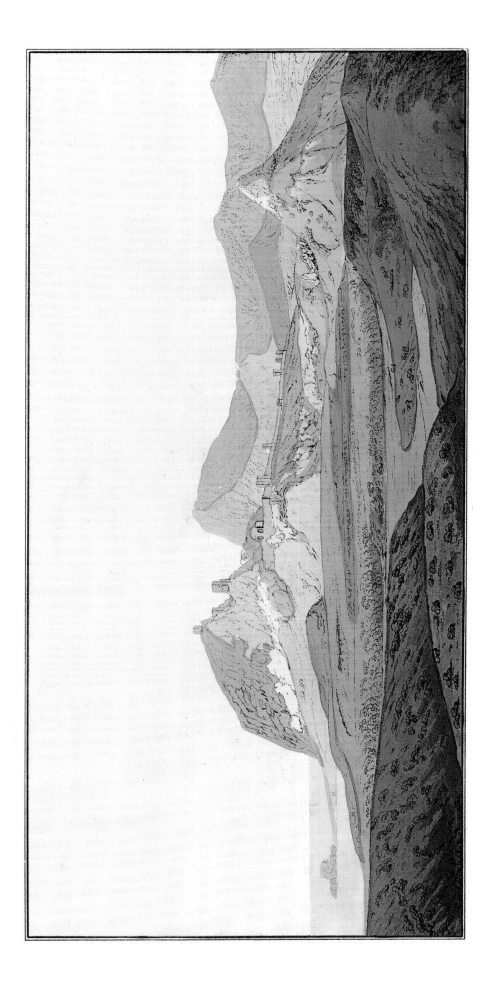

VINEYARDS IN THE VALE OF SUDAGH

MAY 1794

ALONG THE VALLEY OF TARAKTASH THERE are two lofty mountains, the first of which is above the village of the same name, with projecting rocks of breccia, in a crested shape, whence it has received the name of Taraktash, or Cock's-Comb Rock. The other is in an opposite quarter, and consists of a grey calcareous mineral, and is denominated Baka-tash, or the Frog's Rock, on account of a detached stony mass being in a manner suspended on its bare and steep back so as to resemble at a distance the figure of a frog in a sitting posture.

The vale of Sudagh is justly celebrated for its beauty and for its excellent wine. It extends from the shore to the mountains, being upwards of three versts in length and two versts in breadth where it is divided by an intervening eminence named Hydatly, and then continues in a more contracted shape towards the northern village of Taraktash to the additional length of three versts. Throughout its whole extent it is embellished with orchards and vineyards; only the lower part of the dale, which forms an oval surface perceptibly declining towards the south, is exposed to the full sun and produces a wine of superior quality, as, on the contrary, the upper and narrower glens that partly slope towards the north, and are partly deprived of the morning or evening sun by the adjacent hills, afford a harsher liquor, which scarcely holds the fourth place among the wines of Crim-Tartary.

The schistous mountains are remarkable on account of their beautiful and peculiar plants. We met with an elegant white-flowering *Hedysarum*, the *Astragalus lanatus* and *Dracocephalum cuniloides*; the *Cheiranthus odoratissimus* and *Astragalus utriger* (*macrocarpus*), which grow in no other parts of the Crimea. We also saw the *Onosma Tauricum, Herniaria hirsuta, Hedysarum Tauricum, Seseli gummiserum, Salvia Habliziana, Scutellaria orientalis*, with yellow and red blossoms, *Verbascum Graecum, Scabiosa gracilis, Centaurea Picris, solstitialis* and *montana, Echium altissimum*, and many other rare and beautiful plants.

The accumulated rocks of Taraktash with the village of the same name and its gardens in the foreground.

SPRING FLOWERS IN THE PLAIN OF KARASSUBASAR

MAY 1794

THE ENVIRONS OF SYMPHEROPOL (AKMETSHET) AS far as Karassubasar present extensive level country between the calcareous eminences. In the spring these plains are generally embellished with flowers of various shades, and in such abundance as to exhibit at a distant view whole flats overspread with the blossoms of the prevailing plant, according to the nature of the soil. Thus for instance the peony or the poppy produce a bright red veil over the soil; the periwinkle or the *Salvia* make a perfect blue; the *Euphorbia Vaillantia* or the *Ranunculus* are entirely yellow; the *Asphodelus Tauricus (Tauridan asphodel)* or the *Myagrum* appear whitish green; and the tracts of such colours, being alternately relieved with green, afford the most variegated and pleasing views.

The plain in which Karassubasar is erected appears very low. From this town we travelled in a north-easterly, then a south-easterly direction, until, at a distance of 12 versts from Karassubasar, we ascended the ridge of limestone that is formed by the far bank of the Little Karassu river. From the summit of this ridge the magnificent view exceeds all imagination. The whole eminence is composed of horizontal stratifications of limestone, embellished with the finest verdure and rich flowers, as well as a variety of thick woods with oak trees, white beech, lime, linden, trembling poplars, winter and summer pear trees, wild apple and cherry trees, round plum trees, sloes, hazel trees, cornelian cherry trees and water elder.

Our journey now took us eastwards to Kaffa, or Theodosia, which despite its former prosperity and population has lately experienced such adverse fortune as to exhibit now little more than a heap of ruins. It was under the Genoese the principal place in the Crimea; even under the Tartar government it was a populous town flourishing by its trade, but during the late Turkish war, when the Russians made themselves masters of Kaffa, and especially after the occupation of the whole peninsula, this city was almost depopulated.

The ruinous town of Kaffa, or Theodosia, and part of the bay of that name. Among the half-ruined houses there is a Greek church and a large mosque which is in a state of complete repair.

PEOPLES OF THE CRIMEA

I SHOULD LIKE TO MAKE SOME GENERAL remarks on the peninsula of the Crimea. The population of the Crimea formerly amounted to at least half a million. Its first diminution took place in 1778, when in consequence of the peace concluded with the Turks above 30,000 Christians, Greeks as well as Armenians, being at the time settled in Crim-Tartary, were removed to the country between the Don and the Berda, beyond the Sea of Azov. Still more numerous was the emigration of the Tartars soon after Russia had taken possession of the Crimea, from the year 1785 to 1788. During this period, many thousand Tartars, especially in the parts adjacent to the maritime towns, sold their property and goods at the lowest prices and withdrew to Anatolia and Romelia.

The Tartar inhabitants of the Crimea may be divided into three groups: the Nagays, of whom I have already spoken and who, as their features evince, are the unmixed descendants of the Mongolian tribe who formed the bulk of the army of Tshingis-Khan which invaded Russia and the Crimea; second, those Tartars, represented in the plate, who inhabit the heaths or steppes as far as the mountains, especially on the north side, and who in the district of Perekop, where they are still unmixed, retain many traces of the Mongolian countenance with a thinly scattered beard; they devote themselves to the rearing of cattle to a greater extent than the mountain-dwellers, but are at the same time husbandmen though they pay no attention to gardening.

Nearer to the mountains these Tartars, as well as the nobles, are more intermixed with the Turkish race, and exhibit few of the Kalmuk-Mongolian features: this observation also applies to the Crimean nobility in whom those peculiarities are almost entirely obliterated. To the third group belong the inhabitants of the southern valleys, bounded by the mountains, a mixed race which seems to have originated from the remnants of various nations crowded together in these regions at the conquest of the Crimea by the armies of the Mongolian leaders.

A common Tartar with a bullock's whip, and another wearing a cap used in wet weather. The third figure, on the left, represents a shepherd in ordinary clothes.

132

PEOPLES OF THE CRIMEA

THIS THIRD GROUP OF TARTARS DISPLAY a very singular countenance, different from that of all the other inhabitants of Crim-Tartary. Faces of an uncommon length, exceedingly long, and high heads compressed with a view to render them unusually flat, all contribute to produce diversified caricatures, so that the greater part of these persons have distorted countenances, and the least deformed resemble the figures of satyrs. Professor Hacquet, to whom I mentioned this observation during his residence in the Crimea, directed my attention in a letter to a passage in the work of Scaliger: "The Genoese had adopted from the Moors, their predecessors, the custom of compressing the heads of newborn infants about the temples; thus it happens that their children, both in head and mind, resemble the genuine Thersites, though such practice is now discontinued."

I shall not attempt to decide whether these villagers with their singular faces are the remaining descendants of the ancient Genoese who inhabited the Crimea, or those of any other nation that had retired hither. It is further remarkable that the hair and beards of such mountaineers are almost uniformly light brown, reddish, or even flaxen, a circumstance seldom occurring in the Crimea. They are also remarkably distinguished from the common Tartars of the heaths, as represented in the preceding plate, by their costume.

The houses, or huts, of these Tartars are partly formed under ground, being generally constructed against the steep precipices of mountains with one half excavated from the earth or rock and only the front raised with rough stones, having at the same time flat roofs covered with earth. There are among them skilful vine-dressers and gardeners, but they are too idle to undertake new plantations, availing themselves only of those left by their predecessors, especially the industrious Greeks. On the whole, they are at present unprofitable and unworthy inhabitants of those paradisiacal valleys in which they have always shown themselves the first and most ready to revolt against the Russian government.

Two Tartar mountaineers in their everyday dress. In the background are their dwellings, one half of which is excavated into the rock. In the last war with Turkey these Tartars were ordered to dwell 10 versts inland to avoid the danger of their acting as spies and traitors.

PEOPLES OF THE CRIMEA

N THE COSTUME OF THE TARTARS inhabiting the plains there is some variety. Young persons, especially those of noble or wealthy families, dress nearly in the Circassian, Polish or Cossack fashion, as exemplified in the standing figure in the plate, with short, or slit, sleeves in the upper garment. The nobility of more advanced age wear, like the common Tartars, unslit sleeves, and old men suffer the whole beard to grow, whereas the young and middle-aged have only whiskers, as represented in the same plate. Their legs and feet are dressed either in half-boots of morocco or other leather, or they use stockings of the same material, especially in the towns; over these are worn slippers or clogs, for walking abroad; and, in dirty weather, kind of stilt-shoes.

Their heads are uniformly shaved, or at least the hair is cut very short, which they cover with a high cap quilted at the top with cotton and generally green, being edged with black or grey lambskin. The cap is never moved by way of compliment. The clergy and the aged wear under it the fez, or a red, woven calotte. Those who have performed a pilgrimage to Mecca are distinguished by a white handkerchief round the edge of their cap, such being the mark of a *Hadshi*. There are also in the Crimea some Emirs who wear the green fillet round their head. Among the young nobility, however, Circassian caps are the most common head-dress.

The physiognomy of the true Tauridan Tartars bears great resemblance to that of the Turks and Europeans. There are handsome, tall, robust people among them; and few are inclined to corpulency. Their complexion is rather fair, and they have black or dark brown hair. The boys and youth have mostly a pleasing and delicate countenance, to which circumstance, together with the restraints imposed on women, may, perhaps, be attributed the odious propensities prevailing here, as well as in Turkey and Persia.

Two Tartar nobles in their daily dress, and a youth standing in front of them.

PEOPLES OF THE CRIMEA

THE DRESS OF THE TARTAR WOMEN is very different from that of the Nagays: they are in general of low stature, owing probably to their confined treatment in early life, though their features are tolerably handsome. Young women wear wide drawers, a shift reaching to their ankles divided at the front and drawn together at the neck, a gown open in front made of striped silk, with long sleeves and adorned with broad trimmings embroidered with gold; they have also an upper garment of some appropriate colour, with short, thick Turkish sleeves edged with ermine, fur or gold lace. Both girls and married women fasten their gowns with a heavy girdle, having in front two large buckles like those made by the Armenians and Jews of embossed or filigree work, and which were once in fashion among the Russian ladies at St Petersburg and Moscow. Their hair is braided behind in as many loose tresses as it will afford, and is covered either with a small red cap or fez, especially during childhood.

Married women cut off their hair obliquely over their eyes and leave two locks also cut transversely, hanging down their cheeks; they bind a long narrow strip of cloth round the head, within the ends of which they confine the rest of the hair, and turn it up from behind, braiding it in two large tresses. Like the Persians, they dye their hair a reddish brown with Kna. Their undergarment is more open below, but in other respects similar to that of the unmarried, as is the upper dress and girdle. They paint their faces red with cochineal, or other drugs, and white with an oxyd of tin, called *aklyk*, which they carefully prepare over a dung fire in small earthen pipkins. They also dye the whites of their eyes blue with a finely pulverized preparation of copper brought from Constantinople, and by a particular process change the colour of their eyebrows to a shining black. At weddings or other solemn occasions the wealthy further ornament their faces with flowers of gold-leaf, colour their hands and feet as far as the wrist and ankle of an orange hue with kna, and destroy all the hairs on the body with a mixture of orpiment and lime.

Typical female dress in Crim-Tartary. Here are two women in their best but domestic clothes, with no upper garment; the third figure has a white upper gown and her head enveloped in a veil.

PEOPLES OF THE CRIMEA

IN GENERAL, THE TARTAR NOBLES ARE so ignorant that they can neither read nor write, and instead of signing their names they substitute an impression of their rings on which a few Turkish words are engraved. The expense of wearing apparel for the women shut up in their harems is, according to their manner and fortune, little inferior to that of Europeans, with this single difference that the fashions of the former are not liable to change. Even the wives of the common Tartars are sometimes dressed in silk and stuffs embroidered with gold which are imported from Turkey. In consequence of such extravagance and the extreme idleness of the labouring classes, who only exert themselves for procuring the necessary subsistence, there are very few wealthy individuals among the Tartars.

Credulity and inactivity are the principal traits in the Tartar character. To sit with a pipe in their hands, frequently without smoking, for many hours on a shady bank or hill, though totally devoid of all taste for the beauties of nature, and looking straight before them, or, if at work, to make long pauses and, above all to do nothing, constitute their supreme enjoyments. For this mode of life a foundation is probably laid by educating their boys in the harems.

The food of the Crimean Tartars is rather artificial for so unpolished a nation. Among the most esteemed delicacies are force-meat balls wrapped in green vine or sorrel leaves and called *sarma*; various fruits like cucumbers, quinces or apples filled with minced meat, *dolma*; stuffed cucumbers; dishes of melons prepared with spices or saffron, all of which are served up with rice, also pelaw, or rice boiled in meat broth till it becomes dry; fat mutton and lamb both boiled and roasted; colt's flesh is considered a delicacy. Mutton and goat's flesh constitute the food of the common people, together with preparations of milk and eggs; a kind of *pelaw*, made either of dried or bruised unripe wheat, called *bulgur*; their ordinary beverage is made by triturating and dissolving cheese in water, the former of which is called *yasma*, being prepared from coagulated milk, or *yugurt*.

A Tartar and a Nagay musician, the former playing on a common violin, and the latter on a peculiar two-stringed instrument. In the foreground is a small elegant Turkish table, with coffee cups and confectionery. A Tartar merchant listens to the performance.

140

ANIMALS OF THE CRIMEA

THE REARING OF CATTLE HAS ALWAYS, and is still, the principal employment of the Tartars, though more in the lowlands than in the mountains. The inhabitants of the hilly regions, besides sheep and goats, keep in general only one or a few yokes of oxen, that are used by them for conveying fire wood and timber, ready-made wheels, and various kinds of wooden utensils to the market towns. They also possess a few cows, and seldom more than one horse, though many have none, except during the thrashing season. In a few villages situated on the mountains, hairy buffaloes form part of their livestock. On the plains every village has considerable numbers of sheep and black cattle, all are provided with horses and many keep camels.

The Tauridan camel has two humps. It attains here a larger size than among the Kalmuk Tartars, and we observed animals of a white and yellowish white, but less frequently of a black hue. They are seldom used as beasts of burden, but are often yoked to the large four-wheeled waggons, especially on bad roads, and during winter. Opulent Tartars take a pride in conveying their families from place to place, or in travelling to town in covered waggons, drawn by camels. The yoke is placed between their neck and the first hump, and is of a peculiar construction, adapted to the purpose.

From the hair of this animal the Tartar women of the plains manufacture a narrow cloth, which is used in its natural colour, and is extremely warm, soft, and light; if it were made broader it would afford a more lucrative article of commerce.

The breeding of horses is carried on to a considerable extent in the plains, many of the nobles having large establishments and paying great attention to blood. In general, however, there is a deficiency of good male horses for breeding, nor are they properly managed. The horses of the Tartars inhabiting the mountains are small and uncommonly hardy and sure-footed, accustomed as they are from an early age to run upon rocks and dangerous hilly paths, on which account they are sold at a higher price than they are apparently worth.

The Crimean camel with its two humps. In the background is a Tartar village and its gardens.

142

ANIMALS OF THE CRIMEA

THERE ARE THREE VARIETIES OF SHEEP in the Crimea. Those most commonly occurring in the plains are of a middling size, generally white or black, seldom grey and still more rarely brown. Like all the Crimean sheep they have an elongated tail which for half its length is overgrown with fat and covered with coarse wool. In winter large flocks are driven into the mountains, on the Chersonesus, and other places along the sea coast where the falls of snow are slight, so that they find a scanty subsistence throughout the winter, and shelter themselves in cavities of rocks or beneath projecting cliffs.

Of these animals the grey sheep that furnishes the celebrated Crimean lambskins or furs is only a variety; they are produced by a peculiar pasture in the north-western angle of Crim-Tartary, which is by the natives called Tarkhan-Dip, being somewhat less handsome on the peninsula of the Bosphorus, but soon degenerating in other places. A wether of this breed is represented in the plate. Of these handsome grey furs, upwards of 30,000 are in some years exported via Perekop mostly to Poland, where they are in great demand and sold at a high price. Lastly are the mountain sheep, which are much smaller than those of the plains, but are celebrated on account of their fine soft wool.

No province of the empire is more favourable to the rearing of sheep than Crim-Tartary, nor is any better adapted by nature, especially for such as are not stationary, because in the summer they may visit the plains and the cool alpine pastures of the Yaila and in the winter the southern valleys that are free from snow, or the level tracts along the sea coast, and because the winters are in general so mild they may constantly remain in the open air.

The breeding of goats is likewise considerable in the Crimea, particularly on the mountains, and is also profitable on account of the dearness of the skins which are used for manufacture of morocco leather. The fine wool that may be obtained in large quantities by combing them in the spring is not collected by the indolent Tartars.

A full-grown grey Crimean sheep belonging to the breed with diminutive fat tails.

144

RETURN TO MOSCOW

JULY 1794

O N 18TH JULY 1794 I AT length set out on my return to St Petersburg, directing my route towards Koslof, in order to visit this ancient, bustling, commercial town, which still possesses a considerable population.

The town lies 16 versts from Akmetshet, on a gently rising eminence. The heat here in the summer is intense even during the night, and vermin are numerous. It may also be attributed to the same cause that the fevers arising from sudden changes in temperature are not common. The town, with the exception of some desolate heaps of ruins, and the old fortification, is well inhabited; but it is for the greater part built after the manner of the Tartars, in crooked, narrow streets with the houses concealed behind the walls of the courtyards. The great mosque, after that of Kaffa, is the largest in the Crimea. From Koslof to Perekop we travelled over a level steppe, during the summer an arid, barren and dusty tract.

From Perekop we travelled to Kherson, which commands a view of the broad marshy fen which was covered with tall yellow flags (irises). When the wind blows from that quarter it receives a considerable portion of pernicious air during the summer. Among the inconveniences to which this town is exposed is the dirt prevailing in the winter and the insupportable dust, clouds of which are wafted about in every direction during the summer, not to mention the innumerable swarms of gnats that infest it from the marshes. On 25th July, although the heat was almost intolerable, I proceeded on my journey from Kherson over gently rising steppes to Kopenka, where all the water was evaporated, and arrived at night at Nicolayev. This would become one of the handsomest and finest towns of the empire if the erection and embellishment of it were continued with the same spirit with which they were commenced in 1791.

From Nikolayev I travelled to Pultova and then via Akhtyrka, Sumi, Mtshensk, Kursk, Orel and Tula to Moscow. I am induced thus abruptly to terminate my observations, as beside these handsome towns rebuilt to a modern plan few remarkable objects occurred along my route.

A peasant and girl of Russia Minor, in their summer dress, and an old woman of the same country.

SECTION III

RUSSIA AFTER NAPOLEON

AFTER THE DEFEAT OF NAPOLEON IN 1812, Russia lay bleeding in her victory. Robert Johnston arrived to see the smoke-blackened ruins of Moscow, with villages razed and French soldiers plodding wearily homeward through the forests and plains that had been some of the bloodiest battlefields in history. The sights seen by travellers to Russia at that time were appalling, and between his descriptions of them Johnston ruminates the lessons that the tyrant's downfall should teach mankind.

Johnston writes fluently; the images he conjures up are powerful; his language is vivid and he relishes, entertainingly enough, yet rather coldly, his descriptions of people: the German policeman whose "soul is centred in a tobacco pipe", for example, or the Russian who, scrubbed clean after a session in the public baths, nevertheless dresses again in his filthy clothes and is then seen "commencing hostilities against his manifest associates" – the vermin that inhabit his sheepskins. Although Johnston is horrified by the devastation that he finds all around him on his travels, he also takes delight in much of what he sees, and describes the beautiful and the ugly with equal relish.

He starts his journey in the spring of 1814 in Denmark, a country he admires, then continues along the Baltic coast to Hamburg, which has suffered at the hands of both the French and the Russians. His journey then takes him to Stralsund and into Pomerania, across flat marshy country with the Baltic stretching away to the north and the towns of Corlin and Dantzick (Gdansk) rising up from the featureless plains. He crosses the Vistula, and travels to Frauensburg, where he deplores the morals of the inhabitants: "The theatre had been repeatedly burnt down, and money was immediately subscribed to rebuild it; but if a church were destroyed it remained in ruins."

At Konigsberg he sees a group of wretched French prisoners – "the description of their return during the winter from Russia is a frightful picture of the horrors they suffered from the severity of the climate. Many of these men are without fingers and toes and they exhibit large blotches on their faces." From Konigsberg he travels to Tilsit, and then to Memel where he boards a boat sailing for Cronstadt. He sleeps in the hold in a hammock slung from the beams, and "despite the lack of beds or blankets the motion of the vessel rocked us from side to side and the bubbling noise of the passing waves lulled us to sleep." The voyage along the gulf of Finland took eight days, and then Johnston arrived at St Petersburg.

Like all foreign visitors he is transfixed by the beauty of the city, and gives rapturous descriptions both of the whole spectacle and of individual churches, palaces and streets. He also provides us with portraits of some of the people – the market traders, the Russians in the street – and concludes that "every thing appears in the extremes of finery and rags".

The next stage of his journey is the road to Moscow across wilds "which have scarcely been trodden by the foot of man". He arrives in the Holy City to find it in ruins, except for the numerous churches that have survived the flames better than have the houses, of which few are left standing. Then comes "the dark and dreadful part of our journey", through the desolate battlefields of Borodino and the war-ravaged town of Smolensk. He reaches Borisoff, where the French army passed on the day before the battle of the Berezina. He muses, "Here they passed their dreadful nights, a prey to hunger, misery and cold, their only canopy the leafless tree, their only lullaby the drifting snow, which rocked them to their wretched sleep." With these sombre, yet characteristic reflections, Robert Johnston ends his journey.

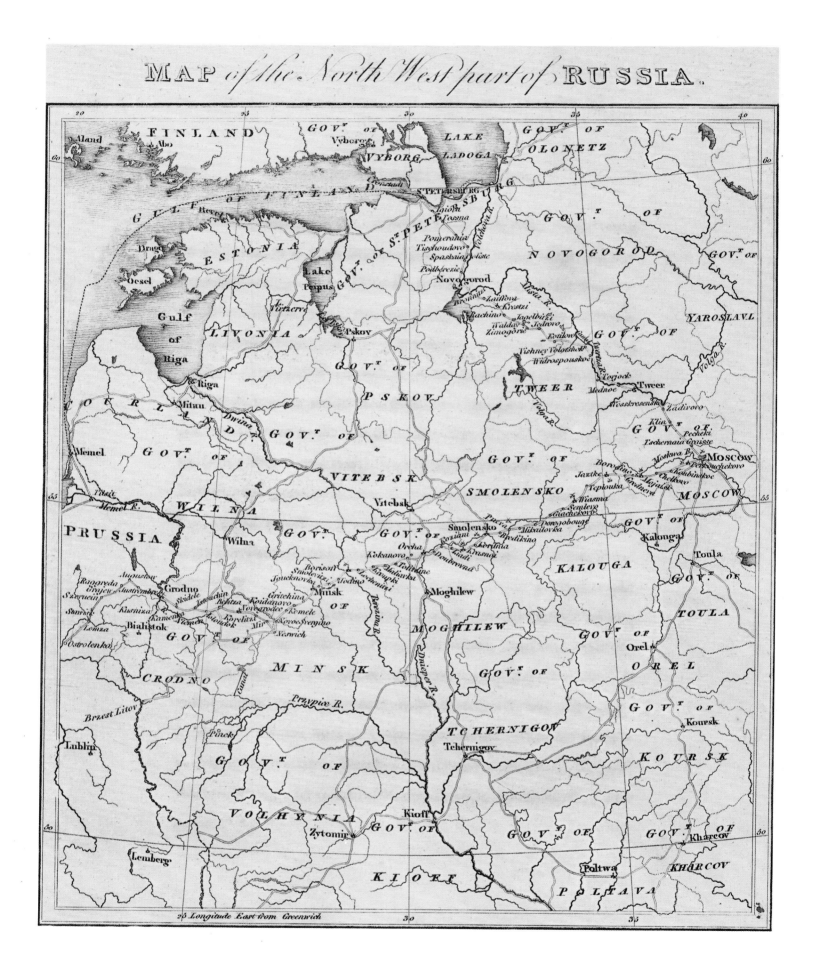

MAP *of the North West part of* RUSSIA.

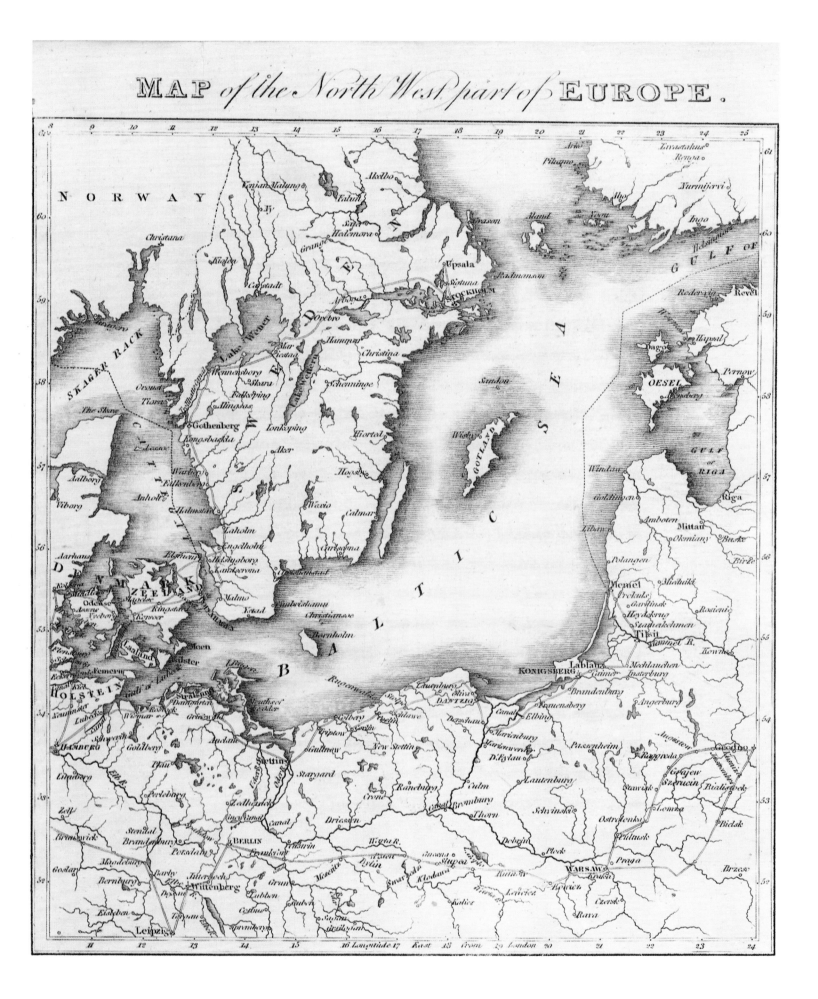

MAP of the North West part of EUROPE.

THE NOBLE CITY OF COPENHAGEN

SPRING 1814

AFTER A SHORT RESIDENCE IN DENMARK, having made the necessary arrangements for our journey to the Russian empire, we took leave, not without regret, of our Danish friends. It is not my object here to attempt to illustrate a nation so well known as Denmark, nor a metropolis so splendid, whose features have been so often portrayed, as Copenhagen, where elegance of taste, social virtues, and the most liberal institutions of charity, equally claim the attention, respect and admiration of every stranger.

Yet we cannot but behold, in this little nation, a striking instance of the mutability of events. The Danes were the greatest people of the north, after the destruction of the Roman Empire, and continued, for a length of time, to plunder, destroy, and even to give laws to, countries now the first in the world. When it had risen to the plenitude of its power, and its flag rode triumphant from the Baltic to the Mediterranean seas, a combination of commercial towns under the name of the Hanseatic League opposed its daring outrages, and overcame what all the powers of Europe could not effect: from that time Denmark gradually diminished in power, wealth and territory.

The winter had been unusually severe, but towards the end of May it had disappeared: spring now burst out in all its brightest bloom; the woods assumed a new form; the meadows sported their varied charms; and, on all sides, was seen the delicate and endearing forget-me-not covering the rude soil with its virgin leaf, and spreading a beauteous carpet over the face of nature. It is impossible for the traveller in these regions not to notice those singular fluctuations of season which seem to separate the spring and winter from each other. The leafless tree may be seen today in all its withered form; tomorrow, clothed in all its richest foliage. The birth of vegetative life seems as sudden as its decay; that beauteous and lingering approach, by which the joys of spring are so truly felt in England, is here quite unknown. The lakes and rivers, and even the sea, are covered with ice half the year, and nature reigns in all the varieties of sublime disorder.

Copenhagen from the gardens of the Fredericksberg Palace. Now, while war has ravaged and left the fairest part of Europe almost a desert and a race of men returning to barbarism, this city represents freedom, riches and the flowering of art and science.

A WAR-RAVAGED LAND: COPENHAGEN TO HAMBURG

SPRING 1814

FROM COPENHAGEN WE PROCEEDED THROUGH HOLSTEIN to Hamburg; thence along Pomerania, and the shores of the Baltic towards Dantzick (Gdansk). It is here that the iron hand of invasion has laid its coldest and most cruel grasp; these are the spots which give colour and character to its sad and melancholy picture. The first city here which is worthy of notice, and the first we arrived at, was Hamburg.

This city fell a sacrifice to the treachery of the Danes and the inactivity of the Swedes, but not before it had made a most gallant resistance. The French army then kept possession of the town for 11 months, and after a loss of 22,000 men made an honourable capitulation. The French will ever be execrated for the cruelties they have committed. To prevent the approach of the Russian soldiers not only the villas of the rich and the villages of the industrious, but even the humble cot of the peasant, and the aged avenues of trees, formerly the admiration of travellers, have all been erased from the earth, and exhibit a shocking scene of ruin and desolation.

As a city Hamburg has neither claims to beauty or regularity. The streets are narrow, and in general intersected by canals of stagnant water. From the nature of its republican government, and the general influx of foreign merchants, but perhaps, more particularly at this time, from the recent effects of its invasion, it presents a varied group of strangers, and occasions a difficulty in fixing the decided character of the place. Here no sovereign is acknowledged; neither precedency nor prerogative above that of a citizen. Title and rank are avoided, in consequence of which an intrusive familiarity is allowed to prevail. The amusements and recreations of the town consist in theatric exhibitions, dancing and tobacco smoking.

Attached to the division here are several regiments of Cossacks and Bashkirs; a race of men worthy of presenting terror in their very looks – they are the most irregular of soldiers, and, in appearance, the most shocking ruffians which the imagination can picture.

Hamburg from the south. The principal and most commanding buildings of the city are the churches: because of the remarkable height of the spires and the extreme flatness of the surrounding country they can be seen at a great distance.

JOURNEY THROUGH POMERANIA

SPRING 1814

THE DISTANCE FROM HAMBURG TO LUBECK is about 45 miles; the road is probably one of the worst in Europe, and though our carriage was easily hung yet from the number of loose stones and inequalities together with the insufferably bad driving of the postilions it was almost impossible to bear the fatigue.

From Lubeck we entered the principality of Mecklenburg in Lower Saxony, and then passed into Swedish Pomerania. The country towards Stralsund is remarkably flat, and in general covered with fine, loose, drifted sand occasionally relieved by small plantations of oak and fir. The roads can only be considered as tracks, and the average rate of posting does not exceed three miles an hour, besides the loss of time a traveller has to expect in procuring horses at the different stages. The posting is under the regulation of the government, and the postilions wear the respective livery of their countries. Each postilion has the appendages of a horn and tobacco pipe suspended from his neck. The first he uses to announce the arrival and departure of a traveller. The other is constantly fixed to his mouth, except when he shares his enjoyment between it and his schnapps.

Before we entered Prussian Pomerania we could not avoid remarking the rigour with which the Swedish laws were enforced. The hideous deformity of the Bonapartean code of police has crept in and reigns throughout. Though now in a period of profound peace, and at a moment when all military barriers should be levelled with the fallen usurper, in this country alone it is retained. Passports though now granted to travellers as a matter of form are here considered of the utmost utility. Nothing can appear more contemptible than the appearance of a wretched town, encompassed by a ditch, with scarcely a gun to defend it, refusing admittance to the traveller without the formal ceremony of obtaining the permission of a *maitre de police*, an animal whose soul is centred in a tobacco pipe and whose honour and integrity is the *pretium argenti*.

Stralsund, the capital of Swedish Pomerania, is strongly fortified both by nature and art, and is surrounded on one side by an arm of the sea and on the opposite by two small lakes which have been joined.

156

A LAPLANDER

THE COUNTRY INHABITED BY THIS RACE of people lies in a very high northern latitude, and has but a scanty population. The inhabitants derive their subsistence from pasturage, from hunting, and from fishing. Those who are chiefly fisherman live upon the borders or in the neighbourhood of lakes, at least during the summer, but in the winter when they are unable to fish they retire to the mountains and forests for the purpose of hunting. They all possess a herd of reindeer which afford them food and are employed in drawing their sledges.

The Laplanders are, in general, of a moderate stature, flat-faced but with rather high cheekbones; their eyes are not prominent, their beard is thin, their hair in general dark brown, and their complexion a yellowing brown arising from their great exposure to the air and to smoke in their cabins. They make use of no linen in their dress: the men wear tight trousers or pantaloons that reach down to their shoes, which are made of untanned leather and are pointed and turned up at the toe. Their jackets are also made quite close, but open on the breast, and their outward garment or coat has tight sleeves and flaps, which reach to the knee. They fasten their coat with a girdle, ornamented with pieces of tin and copper of a yellow colour. From this girdle they suspend their knives, implements for making fire, and pipes for smoking. The different parts of their dress are made with skins and woollen cloth, ornamented with copper and tin, but the cloth is always bordered with some skin. Their caps are high and pointed, and the four seams are covered with cloth of a different colour from the cap itself.

In the plate is a man with his fish in one hand and his nets in the other.

A FEMALE INHABITANT OF LAPLAND

THE WOMEN OF THIS COUNTRY ARE rather short, but in general well made. Their disposition is mild and obliging, but not too free; yet they possess an extreme degree of irritability; a spark of fire falling near her, an unexpected noise, or the sudden appearance of a strange object, will often make a woman faint, or else rouse her almost to a state of frenzy. Their employment consists in making lines for fishing, in drying fish, in milking the reindeer, in making cheese, and in tanning skins. They prepare the tendons of the deer for lines, and they also form a sort of wire or thread of tin by drawing it through small holes made in the horns of the reindeer. They afterwards flatten it, and use it in ornamenting and embroidering different parts of their dress. They also use silver, and a kind of false gold.

The dress of the females is nearly similar to that of the men, but the flaps of their coats are larger and longer, and their girdles, to which they hang their knives, are embroidered with tin thread. The collar of their coats is much higher than that of the men's; they also wear handkerchiefs and small aprons, made of painted linen. They put large silver rings in their ears, and suspend several rows of silver chain from one ring to the other. Their bonnets are generally folded like turbans, and ornamented either with tin or borders of different coloured cloth.

A PEASANT OF FINLAND

THE INHABITANTS OF RUSSIAN FINLAND WERE formerly very similar to those of Lapland, and have indeed the same origin; but they are much less rude and barbarous. Those of the towns are engaged in commerce and various trades, while the inhabitants of the country follow agriculture, hunting and fishing. The latter are laborious, and in general very prudent. Their dress also is similar to that of the Swedish peasants. They most commonly let their beards grow; some, however, only wear moustaches. Their clothes are generally made of a coarse kind of cloth which is manufactured by the women; but they sometimes purchase a finer sort. In winter they wear pelisses, made of sheep or other skins. Some wear shoes made of skin, some wooden shoes, and others make their shoes of the bark of some tree, laced together. They wear a leather girdle, generally untanned, in which they carry a large knife. Their hair hangs loose, and they cover their heads with a sort of felt hat.

A FEMALE PEASANT OF FINLAND

THE WOMEN OF FINLAND ARE NOT in general so handsome as those of Lapland, but their dress is more curious. They wear linen next their skin, sort of drawers, stockings of different colours, and shoes. They also use a kind of slipper, that only covers the heel, the bottom of the foot and their toes. They have a gown, formed like a shift, not very long, but large, without sleeves, and not made to their shape; their external garment, however, has very large sleeves. They also wear short aprons, painted in various colours, and embroidered and decorated with beads and fringe. They cover their heads with a piece of linen, which falls down on their shoulders, and they ornament their throat and neck with several rows of glass beads of different colours and shapes, while similar trinkets hang from their ears. Their girdle goes twice round the waist, and ties on one side; it is made either of skin or linen, is three inches wide with fringe at the ends. In winter the chief part of their dress is made with coarse cloth, as seen in the plate.

A WOMAN OF FINLAND

THOSE FEMALES WHO CAN AFFORD IT dress in rather a more expensive manner in the summer, at least on particular occasions. Their jacket and petticoat are made of linen, embroidered all over with different colours, and made with the greatest art and nicety. The short gown or jacket is rather longer than common, and trimmed round the bottom with a different colour; it reaches to the knees, and in front is ornamented with beads. Their aprons are also longer than common, painted in different colours and patterns, embroidered and richly decorated. Their girdles are studded with ornaments, made of polished iron or yellow copper, and are fastened in front by means of ribands.

They wear various rows of mock pearls round their necks, while several ribands are drawn through their large earrings and fall down on their shoulders. The sleeves of their shifts, which are very large and short, are embroidered in different colours. Their heads are bound round with long handkerchiefs, fastened behind, the ends of which fall down to their heels. Under this head-dress there is a band of skin about four inches wide which covers their hair. This is studded all over with small shells and beads, and is also fringed at the ends.

ALONG THE SHORES OF THE BALTIC TO DANTZICK

SUMMER 1814

THE GENERAL FLAT APPEARANCE OF THESE countries is remarkable. The surface consists alternately of sandy plains and marshes, to which the only interruption is a narrow ridge of clay-marl near Corlin, from whose summit a prospect, boundless as vision, is beheld. The broad expanse of the Baltic is seen stretching along its flat and sedgy shores, while the little town of Corlin appears below surrounded by its extensive plains.

It is surprising to find the unequal distribution of the population throughout this country. Instead of the farmers residing in the country, they generally collect together in villages or in the towns. By this means the countryside appears to be unpeopled. Nothing can be more offensive than the closeness and stench of the houses; let the weather be never so hot, not a window is opened nor a room ventilated. Every apartment has its huge downy beds, and filth is in every corner. No deference nor attention is paid to the stranger in this country; whether he rides in a carriage or in a waggon he meets with the same cold reception.

As we approached Dantzick (Gdansk) we could not but behold with pleasure the beauty of the surrounding scenery. On the north side, a broad and sheltered bay stretched towards the mouth of the Vistula, while a beautiful avenue of trees, about four miles in length, conducted us to the suburbs. The French kept possession of the town during five years. The history of the last years of the situation of Dantzick will be long remembered in the annals of its sufferings. The Russians surrounded the town and prevented all egress. The inhabitants suffered every privation. The cruelties of the French within the walls and the destructive necessity of the Russians in the suburbs completed the scene of wretchedness and horror. Provisions became so scarce that horses, dogs and cats were the only subsistence of the common people. The account of the vices of the French here is shocking. While it stamps a disgrace on their moral character, it plainly appears to have left a strong infection on that of the people.

The monastery of Oliva, near Dantzick. In the intestine revolutions of Poland it was seven times demolished, yet as constantly restored. Once again it is the victim of political disturbances: before the French invasion there were 70 fathers; only 14 of them survive.

ACROSS THE VISTULA TO
FRAUENSBURG AND KONIGSBERG

SUMMER 1814

IT BEING NOW THE BEGINNING OF July the weather was so oppressively hot that we proposed to travel during the night in order to avoid the excessive heat of the day.

Nothing could be more miserable than the appearance of the Poles whom we encountered in the villages. Some of them were afflicted with that offensive disease, the *plica polonica*, or matted hair. The hair hangs over their necks in thick and clotted lumps. The disorder is supposed to proceed from a viscous humour exuding from the head into the tubes of the hair, which dilates to such an extent as to admit small globules of blood. The wretched appearance of the people excited no other feeling than disgust and pity.

We crossed the Vistula by ferry. Its stream is dull and muddy, the banks low, and covered with sedges and brush willow. From the ferry the road crosses the marsh to Marienburg, a small town of ancient respectability; from Marienburg to Elbing the country is a continued flat, insipid morass. The local people here of the lower orders not ungracefully fold a black kerchief round the head, tied in front into a knot. Their appearance and manners are more pleasing than the intrusive immorality of those at Dantzick.

At the wretched village of Truntz, the first stage from Elbing, we left the territory of West Prussia and entered that of East Prussia, in Prussia proper. The second stage brought us to the beautiful town of Frauensburg, celebrated as the residence of Nicholas Copernicus the astronomer.

We travelled to Konigsberg, the situation or appearance of which is by no means inviting. The site of the town is somewhat lower than the surrounding country, which is flat and cheerless; the streets of the city are irregularly planned and badly paved. The morals of the people are similar to those of other fortified towns which have been a prey to invasion. The theatre had been repeatedly burnt down, and money was immediately subscribed to rebuild it; but if a church were destroyed it remained in ruins.

An east view of the town of Frauensberg. The town is partly built under a sandy ridge, which stretches in a parallel line with the bay.

A WOMAN OF ESTHONIA

THE COUNTRY INHABITED BY THESE PEOPLE is in the government of Revel, and not very far from Finland; and indeed they are in many respects similar to the Finns. The men are in general of a melancholy disposition, arising probably from the oppression under which they live, their poverty, and the hardships they suffer under a cold and severe climate. The women feel this oppression much less than the men, and are deficient neither in beauty or vanity.

The dress of the men is similar to the Finlanders, only they do not wear beards. That of the women is singular and rather handsome. They wear stockings and shoes or slippers. Their shifts are white, with large sleeves that reach to their wrists; over this they wear a kind of corset which has a singular appearance from their mode of ornamenting it; it reaches only to the top of the petticoat. Their aprons are long, and have a border about six inches wide; their petticoat has, also, a wider border all round it. This border is made of a different coloured stuff, and is differently ornamented. The bonnets of the married and unmarried women vary. Those of the former, as in the plate, are small, and fit close to the head, are painted with flowers and trimmed with silver or gold. They have a bow, or cockade, behind, from which a number of different ribands fall down on their shoulders. They also wear several rows of glass beads round their necks, and earrings of the same materials.

AN ESTHONIAN GIRL

THE PECULIARITY OF THE DRESS OF an unmarried woman of Esthonia is confined entirely to her head-dress. The bonnets of the girls are without any crown and consist merely of a band round the head higher in front than behind, made of some stiff material, and covered with coloured cloth. They are also tied behind in bows of different colours, and have ribands hanging down from them, but these ribands are confined to a certain number and a certain length. The shifts of all the women are bordered as well round the bottom as at the wrists, and their corsets, as mentioned before, are very odd and fantastic, sometimes made of linen of different colours and embroidered. They wear various coloured girdles, handsomely worked, which go round their waists just above the hip.

FRENCH PRISONERS AT KONIGSBERG

SUMMER 1814

A PORTION OF THE FRENCH PRISONERS FROM Russia are now passing through Konigsberg on their return to France. Nothing can exceed the wretchedness of their appearance both in dress and looks – many of them have only the covering of a tattered blanket, and scarcely any possess the comforts of either hat, shoe or stocking. The description of their return during the winter from Russia is a frightful picture of the horrors they suffered from the severity of the climate. Many of these men are without fingers and toes, and many exhibit large blotches on their faces.

We proceeded from Konigsberg through a flat but beautiful country, well cultivated and diversified with trees and shrubberies. The houses here are rudely built of wood, neither so large nor so comfortable as those in West Prussia. The inhabitants are chiefly Jews, who reside in the country and cultivate the land. Their figures are tall and thin, with a huge unshapely beard; over their persons is wrapped a long loose black cloak and on their heads is worn a black velvet cap and over it a large one of fur.

Around Tilsit is seen the most productive land in this country. The soil throughout is dry soft sand, which occasionally varies into a mixture of clay-loam. The crops of barley and oats grow most luxuriantly, and the produce is far beyond the consumption of the country, so an immense quantity of grain is therefore annually exported. The second stage from Tilsit is remarkably fascinating, and must gratify every admirer of rural nature. The road is flat, smooth, and shaded on each side by aged willows, trained to grow in an outward direction; the extensive plains appear as a soft lawn, covered with the richest verdure, on which securely graze its numerous flocks; while the humble cottages, under the shades of trees, afford a general scene of calmness and retirement. Here the parade of wealth does not intrude: the humble hut does not retire to give room to the stately palace.

Tilsit stands on the west bank of the Memel; it consists of two streets, badly paved, with a collection of mean brick and wooden houses. The river is crossed by a floating bridge of boats, which is removed in winter to allow the passage of the ice.

VOYAGE FROM MEMEL TO CRONSTADT

SUMMER 1814

HOWEVER AGREEABLE THE JOURNEY FROM TILSIT to Memel might appear, yet the instant the latter town is approached all softness of ideas is overturned, every object of picturesque beauty vanishes, and nothing is beheld but a wretched town, surrounded on one side by a wilderness of loose sand and on the other by the sea.

The greater part of this country is peopled by the descendants of the ancient Lithuanians, though considerably intermixed with the colonies of various nations which Peter the Great introduced.

The Lithuanians are a coarse, clumsy, and stupid class of people; their ideas, manners, dress, and actions are those of the dullest, heaviest, and most inanimate description. While the poor women are toiling under the hardships of the day, the men idly loiter about the public houses swallowing vast quantities of raw brandy. The quantity of this pernicious liquor drunk by these people is almost incredible. Every house on the road sells spirits. Even the women carry with them a private bottle, and as they meet in the streets or on the road they first salute by kissing each other's cheek, and then apply the bottle to each other's mouths. The women ride on horseback, after the manner of men, with their petticoats tied round the knee. Nothing can be more ludicrous than to see a woman thus mounted meeting another on foot. They stop, salute, and present the bottle to each other with all the grimaces of a complete caricature.

On reaching Memel we boarded a small Russian galliot sailing for Cronstadt. This voyage along the gulf of Finland though pleasant in summer must, in stormy weather, prove both intricate and dangerous. The gulf is extremely narrow and along its course are scattered several small islands and rocks rendering the navigation often hazardous. The water is extremely light and clear, of a sparkling appearance.

On the evening of the eighth day of our voyage we approached the shores of Cronstadt, the grand harbour and naval depot of the Imperial capital. Then, a packet-boat being under way for St Petersburg, we got on board.

The boatmen at Cronstadt are natives of the south-western provinces who, when the ice breaks up in spring, flock to Cronstadt like birds of passage. Their broad open countenances bespeak good humour, but like all untutored people they are easily provoked and revengeful.

A FEMALE PEASANT OF INGRIA

INGRIA WAS FIRST MADE SUBJECT TO Russia by Peter the Great. The character of the inhabitants is not the most reputable; they are, indeed, remarkable for robbery and various species of debauchery, by which they reduce themselves to the most extreme poverty. Notwithstanding this, the females are very curious in their dress, and indeed extravagant, when compared with their means. The sleeves and other parts of their shifts are embroidered and worked in the most laborious way. Instead of petticoats they wear a double apron, which folds over behind but does not quite meet in front. In front, therefore, they wear another, which is very much ornamented with beads and small shells.

They also wear large and singular ornaments in their ears. In the house their head-dress is formed by an immense piece of linen six or seven yards long, which is fastened round their heads, and falls very low down behind. When the peasants dress themselves for walking to any town, they put on a Russian bonnet as seen in the plate. They also put on a large mantle or robe, either of cloth or linen, over their shift, which fastens on their breast by means of some buttons.

AN UNMARRIED FEMALE OF WALDAI

THE TOWN OF WALDAI IS IN the government of Novgorod, and lies on the road between Novgorod-Veliki, or Great Novgorod, and Moscow. It was peopled by the Poles, who were taken prisoners in the reign of Alexis Michaelovitch. The inhabitants, particularly the women, are cheerful and handsome, and retain even to this day something of their original manners and accent.

The country around Waldai is very beautiful and abounds with lakes, many of which contain islands partially covered with wood. The largest of these lakes is the lake of Waldai of which the town commands a very pleasing view. It is about 25 miles in circumference, and contains several islands. The Waldai hills are not of any considerable height; there are, however, none so elevated in this part of the country. They separate the waters that flow towards the Caspian Sea from those which proceed towards the Baltic.

A MARRIED WOMAN OF WALDAI

T HE DRESS OF THE MARRIED WOMEN of this district differs in some respects from that of the unmarried, as can be seen from the plates. The Polish women are certainly handsomer than the Russian, and the mixture of the former race with the inhabitants of Waldai is the probable cause of the superior beauty of their females. In this, and indeed almost every part of Russia, the natives have a very strong propensity to singing, and this not only in simple melodies but the common peasants perform even in parts. The postilions sing during the whole of the stage, the soldiers sing during their march, and the countrymen in the midst of their most laborious employments.

AN ENCHANTED CITY: ST PETERSBURG

ARLY ON THE FOLLOWING MORNING THE proud towers of the Russian capital burst on our astonished sight. Everywhere around us lay palaces, temples, and monuments, and we beheld a city as if reared by magic and designed by the gods. If we consider the rapidity with which this city has been raised, the harlequin transportation by which the reeds of a morass were changed for the spires of a capital, we are really confounded and lost in admiration.

The first and grandest object which will take the traveller's notice on entering the Russian capital is the majestic and deep-flowing Neva. The river is one third of a mile in breadth, deep, rapid and clear as crystal. The streets are long and spacious, neatly paved and remarkably clean. The houses are large and splendid in appearance; they are in general stuccoed in imitation of stone, or painted either yellow or white, with roofs covered with sheets of iron or tin and not infrequently painted green; while the fronts exhibit numerous ranges of windows, balconies, endless colonnades, verandahs and porticos. The numerous and fantastic-shaped domes and spires of the churches, gilded with either gold or silver, dazzle the eye while the ear is as constantly assailed by the jingling of their bells.

The principal church to be seen here is the Kazan, founded as a rival to Rome and named after the government of Kazán, the first province in the Russian empire to embrace Christianity. The inside of the church surpasses its exterior both in beauty and proportion. The roof is arched, richly ornamented with flowers in relief, and supported by 58 magnificent pillars of polished granite.

Beyond the Kazan church is the place allotted for the merchants' shops and the fruit market. There is every kind of shop, but the most numerous and the most disgusting are the vendors of medicinal herbs and drugs which exhibit the lowest and most melancholy picture; their physiognomy and the superjacent filth under which it struggles to peep out make it impossible for the stomach of any other animal than a Russian not to be somewhat put out of its usual arrangement.

The Kazan church, St Petersburg. Here the body of Kutousoff, the late commander-in-chief of the Russian army, is interred. This veteran was the saviour of his country from the invasion of Napoleon.

THE THEATRE AND THE WINTER PALACE, ST PETERSBURG

THE THEATRE IN ST PETERSBURG IS situated near the market, and the exterior is perhaps the most inelegant of any public building in the city. The interior of the house is large, neatly decorated, and well lighted up. The stage, scenery and dresses are equally well arranged, and the performers are by no means deficient in the histrionic art. At present a popular melodrama is performed which is intended to represent the return of the victorious Russian army from the late campaign.

The part of the house allotted to the company consists of the boxes and pit. The first is the private property of individuals, and the last the reservoir of the very refuse of elegance. The pit is an open space, without seats, and where every degree of rank and rude contact is suffered. If a stranger happens once to get wedged in, he will soon lament his unfortunate destiny. All his senses will be engaged in the most distressing state of hostility; the zephyrs of garlic and onions will be constantly hovering around his nose; myriads of vermin will be wafted on their balmy wings to his racking touch, and no longer will the *sesquipedalia verba* of the drama charm his ear.

At the west side of the Admiralty is situated the Hermitage, or winter palace of the emperor. This huge edifice of stuccoed brick forms a square, on each side representing a front, lost in a confusion of pillars and statues of every order. Nothing is so difficult as an attempt to describe these public buildings: no regularity of architectural rules is observed – the exuberance of all is combined to form one confused mass. Here the present emperor occasionally resides; and here the late Catherine gave free scope to the unbridled licentiousness of her reign. Part of the palace forms the Royal Gallery of Painting; in the collection are several excellent original paintings by Teniers, Leduc, Wouwerman, da Vinci, Rembrandt, &c. with the celebrated collections of Crozat and Houghton. The paintings are arranged in separate rooms, with the name and age in which the artist lived affixed to each frame.

The Hermitage, or Winter Palace, St Petersburg. Within the palace are the winter and summer gardens. The first is particularly beautiful, roofed with glass, laid out in gravel walks and planted with orange trees and parterres of flowers, and filled with exotic birds.

EVERYDAY LIFE IN ST PETERSBURG

SUMMER 1814

THE STREETS OF THE METROPOLIS ARE beautifully paved with small round stones in angular squares but which is the repeated labour of every summer. From the severity of the frost in winter, the pavement of the streets is often displaced; none of the streets has the advantage of a footpath. The postilions drive as close to the walls as they choose. Another disadvantage is the want of water pipes to convey the rain from the houses; but which is thrown from the roofs of the houses by water spouts into the middle of the street. The streets are elegantly lighted up at night, with large square lamps each having four wicks and reflectors. During the night the streets are paraded by guards mounted on horseback and in the day by police officers armed with a long pole with an axe fastened to its point.

Every thing appears in the extremes of finery and rags. In the costume of the common people there is little or no variety, they are all clad alike. A long swaddling cloak, either made of sheepskin or coarse cloth, is wrapped round their bodies. In hot weather it is sometimes changed for a coarse shirt and loose trousers, over which the shirt usually hangs, and is fastened round the waist by a sash. The lower part of the face is concealed by an hideous and filthy beard. The hat is also characteristic. Their countenances are open, and full of good humour, but not one, when carefully examined, can be called handsome. They are coarse, yet have something in the general expression which is pleasing. They talk with rapidity, action and grace. In the town they are evidently addicted to drunkenness, gambling and indolence.

From the attention which the Russians pay to the use of the bath a stranger might be induced to believe that they are the most cleanly people in the world; but the very reverse is the case. However often they may wash and scour their persons, yet they never perform the same attention to their dress, which being of sheepskin contracts every sort of filth and vermin; and no sooner does a Russian quit the bath, than he is seen commencing hostilities against his manifold associates.

The "Flying Mountain". This is a singular conical frame of wood raised to a height of 30 or 40 feet, with a grooved railway leading from its summit to a considerable distance along the plain. Each individual, being seated on a low carriage, is then precipitated down the railway.

THROUGH THE FORESTS AND MARSHES
OF NOVGOROD

AUGUST 1814

FROM ST PETERSBURG TO NOVGOROD THE distance is 127 miles, with a population of only 2500 persons. On each side of the road extend forests and marshes, which have scarcely been trodden by the foot of man. On the west side of the road these wilds extend, without interruption, to the great road, leading towards Lithuania. On the north-east it extends much farther, and through a space only known to the animals of the forest.

We could not but shudder at a most extraordinary instance of immorality which is still allowed to take place among many of the wretched and ignorant people. A father marries his son when almost a boy to a girl considerably older; the son is immediately sent to some distant town, to acquire a livelihood, while the parent cohabits with his daughter-in-law, and often presents his son, on his return, with a numerous family. It is to be hoped that proper measure will be taken by the legislature to abolish these incestuous marriages.

Here the men still hold that low insipid rank, where all is on one level, and their dress the never-varying sheepskin. The women here are singularly dressed. A silk kerchief is bound round the head, with the ends hanging down the back, while the body is covered with a green sarsnet petticoat and vest formed into one, fastened under the arms and supported by broad braces from behind over the shoulders. The arms, as far as the elbow, are covered with very wide sleeves, of white linen. A cord is worn tight across the breasts, which it divides into a most disgusting form. Nothing binds the waist: all, from the shoulders, hangs loose. Some have their dress in front trimmed with rows of buttons, others wear a second sort of short petticoat fastened under the arms and which hangs open and wide to the waist. The stockings are padded, and worn as rollers round the legs; which occasions every woman to walk in a very waddling manner.

Females in the government of Novgorod.

A CHEREMISSIAN WOMAN

THE PEOPLE CALLED CHEREMISSI (TCHEREMHISI) INHABIT part of the governments of Kazan, Nizney, Novgorod and Orenburg. Their origin is from the Finns, although their language is now perfectly distinct. They formerly led a pastoral life, but have since imitated their Russian conquerors and cultivate the land. The character of these people for bravery is not equal to the Russians, nor are their women so handsome, so full of vivacity, or so vain; they are not, however, ill made. The men are hardworking, but slow. They possess neither literature, nor even writing; all their history is traditional, and even the division of time by months and years is unknown to them. They never live in towns, but their villages each consist of about 30 houses, constructed entirely of wood.

In winter, when the works of agriculture cannot be carried on, the men employ themselves in hunting, and the women in spinning, and working on the different parts of their dress, which they embroider with wool, dyed by themselves of different colours. It is the custom among these people to purchase their wives, and the common price is from 30 to 50 roubles, about £10, though sometimes £100 has been given; nor do they always confine themselves to one wife. And as the women are obliged to work, it is not uncommon for a father who can afford it to purchase wives for his sons when they are no more than six years old; but the girls must not be above fifteen.

194

A CHEREMISSIAN WOMAN FROM THE BACK

THERE IS NO DIFFERENCE IN THE dress of the married and unmarried women among the Cheremissi, except perhaps that the married women put more work into theirs. They wear a kind of short trousers, reaching to their knees, as seen in the next plate; and instead of stockings they wrap a piece of cloth round their legs and feet; and their shoes are made from the bark of a tree laced together. Over their shift, which is described overleaf, they wear a loose gown or coat, with long sleeves of various colours, and generally lined with a different colour. They frequently make a border, or trimming, of the skin of the beaver.

Their bonnets are conical and high, but do not end in a point; they are made of the bark of a birch tree, covered with skin or cloth, upon which they fasten a great number of small shells, various kinds of glass beads and small silver coins by way of ornament. From the back of this bonnet a long piece of cloth falls down the back and reaches to the bottom of their gown, about three inches wide, and ornamented in the same way as the other parts of the bonnet. Their girdles are made of coloured cloth.

A CHEREMISSIAN WOMAN IN SUMMER DRESS

DURING THE SUMMER MONTHS THESE PEOPLE wear nothing at all over their shift, which, as seen in the plate, does not quite reach to the bottom of their drawers. This shift comes close up to the throat, and down to the wrists; the collar, wristbands, and seams are all curiously ornamented and embroidered with wool of different colours. There is also a large buckle, where it opens on the bosom, and it is fantastically worked round the bottom. Their girdles are of various colours, and tie on one side with the ends hanging down. Their bonnet also is different, and partakes more of the form of the head; it is a good deal ornamented, and turns up in front.

MOSCOW AFTER THE FLAMES

LATE SUMMER 1814

THE LAST STAGE OF THE ROAD to Moscow is almost a track through forests; it is flat and passes through a waste of uncultivated ground, spread over with birch. Nothing can be more barren and neglected than the appearance of this entry to the ancient capital. Over the extensive sandy plain the traveller may choose his own track, until he reaches the barrier gate of the city. The distance from St Petersburg to Moscow is about 520 miles. Only three small towns, Novgorod, Vishnei Volotshok and Tweer, occur in this long line. Miserable wooden villages occasionally fill up the dreariness of a flat uncultivated country, mostly covered with forests and morasses, through which the greater extent of the road passes in a straight line.

Now, before us stood the ancient and once proud seat of the mighty tsars. What a change! Lowly and prostrate it now lies, its crumbling towers falling into decay, its proud banners torn from their burning walls, and scattering their shivered fragments to the hollow winds – its temples torn – its gates demolished – its houses ransacked – its streets laid waste. Here the army of Napoleon Bonaparte spread themselves, as a lawless band of ruffians, sharing the spoils of this devoted city. To this spot were conveyed every thing that could be snatched from the all-devouring flames, and even the helpless mothers and infants came to beg a covering to their nakedness but who, as might be expected, were refused at the point of a bayonet.

The churches of Moscow are its most characteristic feature, and particularly so at the present moment when contrasted with the ruinous appearance of the other parts of this vast city. Many of the churches were injured, some almost destroyed, but the greater number of them escaped the dreadful effects of the conflagration of the city. At a distance, Moscow must present nearly the same form that it once did: numerous painted spires and glittering cupolas and domes seem to cloud the horizon. But between the churches scarcely a house is seen that escaped the all-devouring flames.

View in the Khitaigorod division of Moscow. This city was frequently styled the Holy City, from the number of its religious buildings and the imposing appearance of the priests and mode of worship. But here the extremes of religion went hand in hand with the extremes of vice.

THE TARTARS' TOWN, MOSCOW

THE KREMLIN IS THE CITADEL OR fortress of the town, and easily commands all parts of it. Within these once sacred walls the mighty monarchs of the empire held their court, and here the most dignified ministers of the church shared the pomp and splendour of the imperial regime.

It is impossible to give any particular description of the palaces or riches of the Kremlin; it is only the bare walls, ruinous and deserted, that now invite the stranger's curiosity. When all hopes were banished from the ambitious and discontented mind of the French ruler, and when he found that he could no longer maintain his usurpation of the seat of the tsars, he determined on destroying what he had not the courage nor the strength to defend. The beautiful church of St Ivan fell as the first sacrifice to his revenge. The walls of the Kremlin were next mined; the explosion took place, but from its immense thickness only a part of it was destroyed.

The Khitaigorod, or second division of the city, has been called the Chinese or Tartars' town. Its most singular features are the tradesmen's shops and the market-place. During the sacking of the city this part suffered the most, and temporary buildings have been erected presenting a spectacle of the most frightful description. Everything is coarse and rudely fashioned, except the various attempts at imitation; ingenuity and taste seem to be stationary, and have not changed for ages past. The street appropriated to the rag-shops and tailors is the most extraordinary sight. It is covered with women dressed in tattered silks, squatting on the bare ground, sewing, mending, cutting up or selling. All the various costumes of the nation, and from the east and south, are here displayed – tattered garments of gold lace, ragged cloaks of velvet, and petticoats of coloured silks – hang around the filthy bodies of these women. The manner of working and idling, sleeping and gambling, are wonderfully contrasted. Idleness and sloth, knavery and superstition, are the offensive appearances of this singular place.

This drawing of the Kremlin is copied from a print of Guerard de la Barthe of 1799. From the rigid strictness of the police we were not permitted to take any drawings of the city; so I have given this copy, adding the present pier, and part of the wall destroyed by the French.

A TARTAR OF KAZAN

THE TARTARIAN HORDES WHICH ARE ESTABLISHED in the Russian empire inhabit the northern coasts of the Caspian and Black seas, the north of Mount Caucasus, and the extensive tracts which lie to the east of the river Ural as well as along the southern part of that river, the mountains and southern parts of Siberia, and the adjacent country. They are also in the governments of Kazan, Orenburg and Tobolsk. The external appearance and character of the Tartars of Kazan are very uniform and regular. They are seldom very tall, and in general rather thin; their faces are small, their complexion fresh, their mouth and eyes less than the common size, the last being generally of a dark colour, and their look lively and striking. They are well made, of a lively disposition, yet timid and modest.

The Tartars of Kazan occupy themselves in commerce, which they carry on by exchanging one sort of merchandise for another, as the use of money is but little known among them. Those who live in villages are employed in the cultivation of the soil. They are also very fond of breeding bees, from which they derive a considerable advantage. This tribe, like most of the Muslim Tartars, shave the head, and leave on the face only a moustache and a little beard around their chin. The head is covered with a leather cap, over which is worn a bonnet with a scarlet crown. The poorer people make their inner habits of a sort of linen, while the rich wear silk, or gold and silver stuffs, with a gown, or coat, made of fine cloth.

A FEMALE TARTAR OF KAZAN

THE FEMALES ARE IN GENERAL MORE remarkable for a healthy and fresh complexion than for beauty. They enjoy a good constitution, and accustom themselves from their infancy to exercise and employment; and their general character is marked by a modest, submissive, and timid behaviour. Those who live in villages employ themselves in spinning wool, making cloth, or in spinning the hemp which they cultivate in considerable quantities. The dress of the married women among all the nations in which the custom of purchasing wives prevails is better and more valuable than that of the girls, for the dress of the wives does credit to their husbands, while that of the unmarried women when they are sold is a certain loss to their parents.

A FEMALE TARTAR OF KAZAN FROM THE BACK

THE DRESS OF THE TARTARIAN WOMEN resembles that of the men in a great many respects, especially in their shifts, jackets, stockings, and boots or slippers, except that the two latter are painted when worn by the females; the fashion also of the shape is a little different. The inner part of a rich woman's dress is embroidered upon the breast, where it buttons; her exterior habit is of fine cloth, sometimes of silk or rich stuff, laced, bordered, and ornamented with gold. Over the upper part of the breast they wear a sort of handkerchief covered with glass beads or small pieces of money, laid over each other like scales. Most women also wear a riband over the shoulder, richly ornamented with beads and gold or silver medals.

They also wear necklaces. Their head is covered with a bonnet, on which pieces of money or medals are placed one over the other like the scales of a fish. To the back of this they fix a strange ornament, as in the plate, which reaches down to the calves of their legs; it consists of a strip of linen three or four inches wide, richly embroidered, and fringed. In summer they dress only in their shift, which is fantastically worked, like those of the Cheremissian women.

THE LEGACY OF WAR: BORODINO AND SMOLENSK

LATE SUMMER 1814

WE WERE NOW TO BID ADIEU to the ancient seat of the tsars. Now lay before us the dark and dreadful part of our journey, the most interesting, but the most melancholy. On all sides lay vast and dreary wilds, their only tracks the bloodstains of war, their only companions the sad remnants of its desolation. The tear of the widow was to awake our sympathy; the cry of the orphan was to din our ears, and send its echo to the listening waste, their husbands, their fathers, and their friends no more! their altars insulted, their homes polluted, and their wretched, houseless, figures stalking abroad, like the genii of famine and despair, and clinging to the yet reeking embers of their roofless dwellings.

Our road was flat, cheerless and insipid, irregularly formed and deeply rutted. We passed by the ruins of villages, sometimes heaps of rubbish, sometimes entirely swept away from the face of the earth.

About 10 miles from the town of Mojaiske we reached the plains of Borodino, where the battle between the Russian and French armies was fought, on 7th September 1812. We could not but gaze with sorrow at the scene before us; one complete mass of destruction and desolation presented itself. The whole is almost a desert. Here the Russian army lost 35,000 men, and the French somewhat more.

We turned away from these melancholy scenes and pursued our journey towards Smolensk. The country gradually became hilly, and partly covered with wood and cultivation. When we came in sight of the turrets of Smolensk, the view was striking and picturesque. The streets seem to hang on the edge of precipices. The alternate rising and sinking of the walls from the unevenness of the ground; the grotesque towers and their rude gothicism; the steeples, mingling with the branches of trees, and the trees concealing the view of the houses; the number of gardens, orchards and groves - altogether form the most picturesque and eccentric group which can be conceived, belying the recent scenes of sorrow and destruction that were witnessed by its unfortunate inhabitants.

Nothing can present a more singular and romantic appearance than the town of Smolensk, yet never did the hand of destruction press more heavily than on this ill-fated city. Everything bears the mark of the French devastation; its fate must ever darken the page of history.

INTO ANCIENT LITHUANIA

OCTOBER 1814

THE ROAD FROM SMOLENSK LED US through a country extremely beautiful, well cultivated and diversified with plantations, somewhat resembling English park scenery.

The commencement of ancient Lithuania is passed at Liadi. We lost the Russian character – the lively and boisterous mirth of the poor Russ became changed for the cold, calculating silence of the Jews. The women are yet more disgusting than the men; they are clad in a most ridiculous and gaudy dress of silken rags; on their head is a large white napkin rolled round, with three tails hanging over their shoulders; and, under this head-dress, a kind of flapping cover of pearls, with dangling steel ornaments, hangs over the ears and forehead. The body is covered with a loose silk vest, and a large petticoat of the same; the arms are hid in long loose shirt-sleeves terminated with a deep worked frill. The shoes are made without leather at the heels, and every one appears slip-shod. Over their dress they wear a large silk gown, and in some instances two, the sleeves of which hang down the back; a fur cloak is suspended from the neck.

All this superfluity of dress is huddled on, in the most careless manner, and the hands seem constantly employed in detaining it on the body. The dress seems a bundle of dirt and rags; there never was a more perfect antidote to love and the graces than a Lithuanian Jewess. They command the men, and reign without control; the mistress of the house reads her prayers every morning, but at the same time walks through the rooms and in the midst of her devotion observes, checks, and roundly scolds at the faults committed.

The native Lithuanians generally wear a white flapping hat, and a white woollen shirt; their legs are wrapped up in pieces of sail cloth, tied with leather strings – the shoes are clumsy, made of the bark of the birch tree. They are a small class of men, with light hair, fair complexions and little or no beard; they are abject, gross, indolent and disgusting, both in their appearance and in their habits.

Lithuanian Jewesses, whose dress is at the same time gaudy and shabby, and worn without grace or elegance.

A FEMALE TARTAR OF THE TRIBE OF TELEOUTI

THIS BRANCH, WHICH IS NOT VERY considerable, of the Tartar nations, inhabit the villages in the district and neighbourhood of Kouznetsk, near Mount Alta. They are in some measure connected with the Kalmuks. That branch of the Teleouti which is subject to Russia have their villages near the banks of the river Tom, and other small rivers that fall into it. Most of these have the manners and character of the true Tartar; some, however, much resemble the Kalmuks.

The females cannot be reckoned handsome, as their complexions are bad, and their faces in general flat. Their manners and modes of life are proofs of an idle, indifferent and insensible disposition. Their minds are uncultivated, and they are scarcely able to comprehend the simplest question, to which they always give the shortest possible answer. Their cattle, their corn, and their children, together with the power of being idle, form all their concern; if they possess these, they are satisfied. They live happily together, are very peaceable in their behaviour towards their Russian neighbours, and pay their tribute without murmuring.

A FEMALE TARTAR OF THE TELEOUTI TRIBE FROM THE BACK

THE DRESS OF THIS TRIBE IS not remarkable for its excellence, though it is made like that of the other Tartars; but these people are in general so poor that they cannot afford to expend much on their dress. The females are the best clothed; they wear rings, or small chains, in their ears; their hair is divided into two or more parts, which they ornament with ribands and small shells. They wear a small flat cap, with glass beads and medals for ornament, and over this a sort of bonnet bordered with fur. The unmarried women generally wear a peculiar ornament from the nape of their necks, consisting of a piece of cloth about four inches wide and 18 long, entirely covered with beads and pieces of money.

They are by no means a cleanly people, their dress is generally very dirty, and their linen covered with grease. Their food is various, but one of their greatest delicacies is horse flesh. Their usual drink is water, but they distil some spirits from corn, and a sort of arrack. It was formerly the custom of these people to burn their dead, or to place them upon some tree in a forest: In this manner they still expose their young children when dead. They partly profess Schamanism, and are partly Muslims.

THE END OF A JOURNEY

AUTUMN 1814

WE ENTERED THE GOVERNMENT OF MINSK, travelling through large forests of fir trees. Nothing can be more distressing to behold than the dreary and desolate tracks through which the French army retreated. The avenues of birch trees which lined this part of the road are entirely burnt down and every tree scorched, not only on the roadside but in the very depths of the forest.

We reached the town of Borisoff, which is a district town and the residence of a governor and a troop of Cossacks. During the last stage of this journey we passed several detachments of Cossacks and Bashkirs, and their wild appearance in these solitary and gloomy forests was indeed terrifying. This was also the stage the French army passed on the day before the battle of the Berezina. What hardships they must have undergone in those dreary scenes, surrounded by the horrors of a Russian winter, may be conceived but cannot be described. Here they passed their dreadful nights, a prey to hunger, misery and cold, their only canopy the leafless tree, their only lullaby the drifting snow, which rocked them to their wretched sleep.

The battle of Berezina completed the destruction of the French army. Only six months before, more than 400,000 chosen soldiers crossed the Niemen to subvert the independence of Russia, and of that number only 24,000 re-crossed the Berezina.

Having now completed the extent of our investigations through a part of the Russian empire, and being on the eve of entering a new kingdom, we could not but contemplate the vastness and immensity of this unwieldy empire, to support whose overgrown size the natives of the most distant and untrodden regions are called in. Hither flock the savage tribes which prowl along the dens of the Caucasus, or the banks of the Oby; the wandering Samoide and the houseless Tartar here find a home and employment. The vastest bounds of the vastest empire in the world pour along their contents like a sweeping torrent; all tend to one point, all flock to one centre, and under the wide waving banners of their mighty mother, all are enlisted, all are to serve.

Borisoff, from which the road crosses a country little cultivated, very moist, and most dreary, covered with forests and dotted with wretched wooden hovels. There cannot be, perhaps, anywhere, more miserable specimens of architecture than the Lithuanian villages present.

A TCHOUVASHIAN FEMALE

THE TCHOUVASHI LIVE IN THE SAME part of the Russian Empire as the Cheremissi, and are of Finlandic origin; they have, however, a peculiar dialect. In other respects they are very similar, and are not more enlightened than their neighbours. The dress of the men is nearly the same, and there is no distinction in dress among the women between the married and the unmarried. In summer they seldom wear anything over their shifts, which are fastened by a girdle and have a fringe or border of a different colour. In winter they wear a robe made either of skin or coloured cloth.

Their bonnets are ornamented with glass beads and pieces of silver money. They wear over their head a piece of white linen, worked and ornamented round the borders with beads, over which they wear their bonnet. Those who are promised in marriage cover their face with a veil but the married women fold this veil back on each side, and fasten it under their throat by means of a ring. In some villages the women never wear bonnets, but a sort of bandeau worked and ornamented with small white or speckled shells. They also wear a broad piece of linen, worked like their head-dress, which fastens to their neck, or back part of the head, and comes down in front almost to their girdle. Their shoes are formed from the bark of a tree, and they wrap a piece of linen round their legs and feet instead of stockings.

A RUSSIAN PEASANT

THE PEASANTS OF RUSSIA, PROPERLY SO called, are moderate in size, and form an active and hardworking race of men. They are in general very healthy, and of a cheerful and kind disposition. The natural simplicity of their manner of living, and their rude, but dry and wholesome climate procure them a degree of physical complacency of which few other nations can boast. Their dress consists of a round hat, a coarse coat of drugget (in winter exchanged for some skin prepared with the wool on) reaching to the knee, trousers of thick coarse linen, a woollen cloth bound round their legs instead of stockings, with shoes or sandals made of bark, and fastened with strips of the same material wound round their ankles. They always wear beards, which are bushy and of various colours.

Their females are marriageable at a very early age, and this is to be accounted for in so cold a climate chiefly by the constant use of the hot bath. It is used by people of every age and in all circumstances, and seems to be so indispensable a necessary to the common people that, whether ill or well, young or old, children at the breast or their mothers, they are constant in the use of it.

The cottages in which the peasants live are not the most commodious: they are square, and formed of whole trees piled one upon another, and fastened together at the four corners; the interstices of them are filled up with moss; the roof is in the form of a penthouse, and covered with the bark of trees, over which they put turf and mould. After the house is finished they cut out the windows and doors, both of which are very small, particularly the former.

ACKNOWLEDGEMENTS

The Publishers wish to thank Pam Opie-Smith and Anne Dunford of The Royal Geographical Society for their invaluable assistance in this project.

The Publishers acknowledge their indebtedness to the following publications which were consulted for reference:

The Atlas of Man (Omega Books, London 1987); *Lippincott's Gazetteer* (1952); *Languages of the USSR* (Matthews 1951); *Administrative Map of the USSR, 1:8,000,000* (1974); *Times Comprehensive Atlas* (1986); *Russia Under Western Eyes* edited by Anthony White (Paul Elek 1972).

Maps on pages 8, 9, 10, 11, 86 and 98 are taken from *The Illustrated Atlas of the Nineteenth-Century World* edited by Montgomery Martin (Studio Editions, 1989).